MICROCOMPUTER APPLICATIONS
in Educational Planning
and Decision Making

C. KENNETH TANNER
C. THOMAS HOLMES

Teachers College, Columbia University
New York and London

Published by Teachers College Press, 1234 Amsterdam Avenue, New York, N.Y. 10027

LIBRARY OF CONGRESS CATALOGING IN PUBLICATION DATA

Tanner, C. Kenneth.

Microcomputer applications in educational planning and decision making.

(Computers and education series)
Includes index.
1. Educational planning—Data processing.   2. School management and organization—Decision making—Data processing.   I. Holmes, C. Thomas, 1948   . II. Title. III. Series.
LB1028.43.T37   1985   371.2'07   84-23952

ISBN 0-8077-2766-0

Manufactured in the United States of America
90 89 88 87 86 85   1 2 3 4 5 6

Contents

Introduction

The purpose of this book is to illustrate some
well-defined planning methods that are useful in planning for education and other public service areas. An
overview of planning concepts, microcomputers, and the
related literature is presented in chapter 1. Following this introduction, twelve planning techniques are
integrated throughout the five remaining chapters.
Each chapter is designed in a systematic, progressive
style whereby the reader may move from simple to more
difficult problems. The book may, therefore, serve as
a learning package, textbook, reference work, or a
guide to programming microcomputers. The reader is not
required to have a great deal of knowledge of research
or organizational and political processes pertaining
to public service agencies. Knowledge of computer
language or high level mathematics is not necessary,
although some quantitative solutions assume a minimal
understanding of high school algebra. All the computer
programs included in appendix A may be copied onto most
microcomputer systems and "saved" with only very minor
changes.[1]

Professionals and students in education, public
administration, planning, and policy research will find
the problems and proposed solution strategies of value
in teaching, research, and applied settings. Most of
the emphasis in this work is on practice. While theory
is acknowledged, the focus is on data collection, problem investigation, and the generation of solutions.

---

1. The microcomputer programs are available on diskette
for the Apple II-e. The diskette may be obtained by contacting
the authors at G-10 Aderhold Hall, University of Georgia, Athens,
GA 30602. The cost is $7.00.

For example: What are the most time efficient ways to
plan and manage a program or project? What are the key
variables that the researcher should investigate in the
community when developing policies for public service
agencies? Which models are best for forecasting student population--the major beneficiaries of local tax
dollars? How should program development take place
and what approaches should be used in the initial
phases of facilities planning? What are some appropriate methods and models for locating sites for public
buildings? These questions frequently confront the administrative planner and policy maker.

   Twenty-eight problems with explicit solutions are
incorporated in chapters 2 through 6. Additional problems with their answers are given in appendix B. Solutions are determined in a straightforward manner that
leads to the use of the software package. Each major
planning model is presented in BASIC, the language most
frequently used in the world of microcomputers. The
necessary input and output per problem are revealed.

   The theme of the book focuses on a basic understanding of how analytical planning methods may be used
proactively to complement the mission of an organization. More emphasis is placed on solving problems and
generating information for planning new policies than
on the evaluation of policies after their implementation. The book deals with practical problems and solutions amenable to planning and decision making.
Throughout the book there are special hints to the
planner on how he or she can expect plans to be received by policy- and decision-making groups. Special
emphasis is placed on long-range planning, since comprehensive planning in advance of policy decisions
should be the concern of every decision maker.

MICROCOMPUTER APPLICATIONS
in Educational Planning
and Decision Making

Chapter 1
Introduction
to Planning Concepts
and Microcomputers

PLANNING CONCEPTS

Let us begin an investigation of planning and
decision-related activities by taking a look at some
conceptual dimensions. It is important immediately to
recognize that the environment where planning takes
place is the most significant variable in the planning
process. Within this environment, planning activities
are accomplished by people--people living within a
political environment where formal and informal organizations exist. The core of any conceptual framework
for planning involves a person or a group who work
through a set of organized activities designed to influence a decision about the future of a person, a
group of persons, an element of an organization, a
total organization, several organizations, or various
combinations of all these targets.

Planning may be categorized as proactive or reactive. Proactive planning implies the anticipation
of a problem before it arises. The results of proactive planning are alternatives that limit negative
consequences and maximize positive consequences. On
the other hand, reactive planning involves individual
or group efforts to solve a set of problems after they
have occurred. The obvious alternative to proactive
or reactive planning is inaction or to do nothing.
Proactive planning is less popular than reactive planning in our political environment because historically we have had difficulty in convincing practicing
politicians of the need to analyze or solve problems
before they arise. According to Quade,[1] an essential
element in planning is the forecast of future events.
We agree with this observation and also contend that
analysis is not planning, although the plan may result

from analysis. Likewise, a plan may not necessarily
result from a forecast.

Conceptual frameworks for planning activities are
not difficult to discover in the literature, yet those
without decision making as a goal appear to be useless
unless one is satisfied to just plan for the sake of
planning. A sound framework for planning rests upon
the assumption that planning is a process of preparing
a set of decisions for future action.[2] If we assume
that action involves an element of change, then planning depends upon attitudes reflecting the desire for
orderly change and strategies that facilitate change.[3]
Within this context we shall acknowledge that the environment influences the knowledge base, the goal
orientation, the strategies for planning, and the implementation of plans. We must not forget that planning activities are accomplished by people, not objects,
who also influence an organization and its environment.
Thus, a complex interactive process is characteristic
of an environment where planning is accomplished.

Inbar[4] has offered a comprehensive two-dimensional
conceptual foundation for planning. The basis of the
foundation is represented by two Cartesian coordinates
where two types of knowledge and two goal orientations
define the axes. Goal orientation is represented on the
x-axis. Allocative planning activities dominate the
right side of the axis, while the left half of the axis
is concerned with behavioral goal orientation. The
y-axis is divided into two components. Explicit knowledge dominates the upper half of the y-axis, while tacit
knowledge influences the lower part. Inbar contends
that most planning activities are allocative in nature.
That is, we plan for the allocation of resources needed
by the people within an organization. This type of
goal orientation is in contrast to the behavioral goal
orientation that is directly aimed at the behavior of
people in an organization.

Within this conceptual frame of reference Inbar's
first quadrant consists of rational planning activities
where patterns of implementation are integrated with
the allocative goal orientation and explicit knowledge.
People within the organization follow a specific course
of action influenced by formal objectives sanctioned
by the power structure. Legislation and coercive mani-
pulation are power sources that are prevalent in this
setting. The second quadrant of the conceptual framework rests upon explicit knowledge and behavioral goal
orientation. Planning strategies are defined as
"mixed scanning" where patterns of implementation depend upon manipulative persuasion and the objects of
planning are the roles and responsibilities of people.
Etzioni[5] developed a mixed-scanning model as a synthe-
sis of incrementalist and rationalist planning that

outlines components of decision making. Human judgment, however, is the key ingredient in any planned implementation.

The third quadrant slips into the mode of incrementalism. The goal orientation is behavioral and the knowledge base is assumed or implied. Implementation of plans depending upon a high degree of value choice is essentially a reeducational process. Trade-offs between facts and values are characteristic of decisions resulting from this component of the framework. Bargaining, push and tug, and trial and error are appropriate descriptors of planning activities in quadrant three. Another aspect of incremental planning not emphasized by Inbar is that this typology places emphasis upon decentralized control whereby things get done through a decentralized bargaining process. Our contention is that problems rarely get solved, yet some analysis is done, a decision is made, new problems arise, more analysis is completed, and so forth. Lindbloom[6] described this as the "science of muddling through."

The fourth quadrant provides a foundation for explorative patterns of implementation that draw from tacit knowledge and allocative goal orientation. The planning strategies employed in this element of the conceptual framework are defined as "linkage planning tactics." The primary question answered with this set of tactics is: What are the impacts and relationships of organization and environment upon the educational or any other organizational process involving people with problems to be solved?

Based on this overview one should recognize that planning is goal oriented. Furthermore it is dependent upon the knowledge base of the planner plus the reactions of those persons affected by the implementation of the plans. Implementation of plans implies decision making founded on some conceptual base. Just how planning activities are accomplished, even if rational, analytical techniques are the central focus, frequently depends upon other elements of a conceptual framework such as mixed scanning, incremental, or linkage. Beyond these, advocacy and radical strategies may often be necessary for implementation of the best laid plans.

Even where a set of complex theories exists, planning should be a course of action whereby a set of organized activities leads decision makers to alternative solutions. The purpose of planning is to facilitate the operation of an organization or a subunit thereof, by establishing goals, objectives, policies, and methods aimed at proactive treatment of internal and external variables. Unfortunately, most planning in the United States is like economic policy; Nanus suggests that it is present-oriented and frequently reactive.[7]

Planning and analysis may or may not precede decision making or policy development. Public policies, according to Lindbloom,[8] may evolve from new opportunities, as well as from problems, and may just happen. The planning strategies discussed in this book are best suited for decision making, research, and generating . information for solving problems before they arise. Although the emphasis here is on rational analysis, there is no attempt to suggest that planning, decision making, social research, and policy development are exact sciences. This was emphasized in the presentation of the four quadrants representing planning activities. The field of policy analysis, for example, is generally thought of as encompassing planning and analysis strategies such as systems analysis and operations research. Quade[9] indicated that policy analysis places emphasis on implementation and governmental organization. Educational planning parallels this concept. Two major phases in the study of public policy, as discussed by Jones,[10] are getting the issues to government and getting governmental action on the controversial public problem. The latter concept leads to research after policy implementation, and the former focuses on analysis before the decision to implement. Again, it is important to point out that our major emphasis in this work is on research in advance of decision making.

By advocating the formal analysis of problems and the planning of alternative decision strategies, we clash with tradition. The notion of the planning process as serial with clusters of unguided activities parallels Lindbloom's incrementalism.[11] Although he places some limited value on analysis and planning, Lindbloom has some serious doubts about the significance of formal analysis in the policy planning process. As a challenge to the incrementalists, Peter House[12] noted that it is the opinion of some that public officials are inept when it comes to decision making and they should rely on the specialists with methods and models for providing analyses for decisions.

As we move into the areas of research and planning for the purpose of solving problems and forming public policy, we note some difficulties. For example, one major concern for the beginning researcher is the wide range of definitions of planning, research, technology, and policy. Policy is frequently used to refer to highly diverse public actions and decisions. Policy, like systems analysis, is a very dynamic term that is frequently ambiguous unless something is known about the problem to which it is addressed. Hence, we read about energy policy, school board policy, defense policy, legislation, statutes, and regulations that may simply be expressions of rules, decisions, or programs. Heclo[13] considers policy as a course of action or inaction and not a set of specific decisions or

actions. This course of action must be viewed through
an environmental and organizational perspective to understand its bounds of influence. Perhaps it is also
wise to know the orientation of the analyst as well.

Concepts of planning, research, technology, and
decision making have a wide scope. For example, the
current literature abounds on topics such as general
educational planning, social and economic planning,
technological planning, policy planning, urban and
regional planning, futurism, and educational facilities planning.[14] These areas represent special academic components and have their own language. All
these various disciplines have a common goal--to make
a positive contribution toward improving the welfare
of people. Organizations representing these areas of
planning and research strive to help solve social and
economic problems.

Throughout each academic discipline, one method
of planning--rational systems--seems to be a common
thread, yet as noted earlier in this chapter, there
are many theories of planning and decision making.
The rational systems method is frequently secondary
to mixed scanning, incremental, linkage, radical, or
advocacy planning in our politically oriented public
service agencies. The rational approach is characterized by a centralized decision-making structure and
assumes ample data. It is goal oriented and most frequently depends on deterministic and probabilistic
models for generating alternatives.[15] The rational
systems method complements the other strategies that
share the concept of transactive planning. The concepts discussed in this book favor the rational systems method tied to transactive theory.

Transactive planning places emphasis on individuals having a voice in their own welfare. New ideas
are always welcomed. Thus, Friedman has stated that
in transactive planning, action validates the contin-
ual evolution of ideas.[16] Transactive planning
recognizes how decisions are made within the organization and permits face-to-face contact with persons
affected by decisions that result from the combined
rational and transactive efforts. When one strategy
(rational or transactive) is used without the other,
there may be trouble at the implementation and operations phases of the planning cycle. That is, people
resist plans that are imposed upon them. In summary,
the rational approach favors decisions that rely on
hard data and analysis, while the transactive theory
allows people who apply subjective judgment in decision making to be in charge of or have a voice in the
quantitative models that generate alternative solutions.

This book, therefore, lends support to the
rational-transactive theory of planning, research,
decision making, and policy development. Table 1.1

Table 1.1.   The Major and Minor Functions of Rational and
Transactive Theories in Planning

Planning Phase	Rational Theory	Transactive Theory
I - Decision to plan	M-	M+
II - Information dissemination	M-	M+
III - Problem awareness	M-	M+
IV - Estimating the scope of the problem through analysis	M+	M+
V - Classifying the solution(s) in terms of goals and objectives	M-	M+
VI - Generating alternative solution strategies	M+	M-
VII - Implementing solution strategies	M+	M+
VIII - Operating under the new strategies	M-	M+
IX - Evaluating progress	M+	M+

Note: M+ = Major functions; M- = Minor functions.

indicates the relationships between the rational and
transactive theories in planning. The decision to ini-
tiate planning activities, if not an ongoing process
already, should be a major function of the people within the organization, since it is assumed that the result of the plan or plans will influence them as well
as society. Under the rational theory this decision
is generally made by one person. Obviously, it is not
implied here that the chief decision maker is left out
of the decision to plan. Certainly someone at the top
of the organizational structure must advocate the move
to plan. There should be policies that support continuous planning efforts within the organization. We
shall assume that information sharing is a chief characteristic of this hypothetical organization. Phase II
indicates that the transactive theory encourages information flow, in both directions, at each level within
the organization. Phases I and II may overlap with
each other and Phase III. This overlap or sharing of
information may produce feedback. Thus, we note that
planning under the rational-transactive theory is,
indeed, interactive and dynamic.
    With Phase III, problem awareness, we assume that
people in the organization are adequately informed so

that the scope of the problem or problems may be estimated (Phase IV). A sound subjective and quantitative data base is needed to establish the magnitude of the problem. Both theories play a major role here since the rational theory assumes ample data and the transactive theory allows face-to-face discussion and subjective evaluation of these data. When the data are analyzed through rational means and then subjectively, we are ready to describe the solutions in terms of goals and objectives. The rational theory makes a contribution in Phase V, but the major contribution comes from the transactive school of thought since people are given the responsibilities of achieving these goals and objectives. The logical phase following the classification of solutions is to generate or seek alternative solution strategies (Phase VI). Again, there is overlap between this planning phase and Phase V since there exists the desire to know hard facts, such as how much the solution will cost. Therefore, more dependence is placed on the rational approach in Phase VI than on the transactive theory.

Equal emphasis on the two theories is needed in implementing solution strategies (Phase VII) because we need people--people who have contributed to the total planning process. We also need the hard, cold facts that are generated under the rational theory. That is, the rational theory helps minimize multiple guessing with respect to the right strategy. Since the new solution strategies must be operated and managed by people, Phase VIII is dominated by the transactive theory. The rational data are needed, however, but the greater need is the cooperation of the total organization and a more decentralized set of responsibilities if the total plan is to be successful. Finally, the evaluation phase (IX) is dependent upon both the rational theory and the transactive theory. That is, most evaluations should depend upon quantitative as well as subjective information. All of these phases are usually necessary for planning and implementation activities. The technological tool (the microcomputer) complements these planning phases and theories as indicated throughout the book.

MICROCOMPUTERS

As we review these planning functions for the purpose of practical application in the world of public service, the following question is posed: Where can computer technology be of greatest assistance in planning, research, policy studies, and decision making? Before we answer this question our point of view concerning the microcomputer should be made clear. We

perceive the microcomputer and technology to be the
servants of persons who are involved in planning, research, and decision making--not their masters.
Hence, the microcomputer is a sophisticated hireling,
where the sophistication is dependent upon the master
as well as the servant.

Based on the planning phases outlined in Table 1.1,
the microcomputer may provide assistance in each of
the nine components that are outlined. Perhaps this
developing technological wonder can render the most
support in the phases of information dissemination,
establishing the scope of the problem through analysis,
generating solution strategies, operating, and evaluating progress. If the microcomputer is used primarily
as a word processor, then its greatest assistance would
be in information dissemination. On the other hand,
if the microcomputer is employed to process statistical
or mathematical models, Phase IV, analysis for the purpose of estimating the magnitude of a problem would
become its greatest contribution. In sum, we emphasize
that the applications of the microcomputer in the field
of education and public service are really left up to
the imagination, sophistication, and tenacity of the
persons in charge of planning, research, and decision
making.

For approximately two decades we have studied and
discussed the implications of computer-assisted instruction (CAI). In 1966 CAI was indeed very popular,
but for reasons such as prohibitive costs and the re-
quirement of large areas for data processing and
storage, the concept was kept on the back burner. With
the developments in technology during the past five
years, cost and storage have been eliminated as constraints on computer use in small jobs and in instruction. Thus, the term "educational computing" is re-
placing terms such as computer-assisted instruction
and computer-based learning.[17] Educational computing
has entered a phase of popularity that has been spurred
by the development of microcomputers.

The concern for the development of packages of
computer programs (software) is with us today, but it
is not as serious as it was in the 1960s. Students
and parents are forcing teachers to learn how to
utilize the microcomputer, and teachers, students,
and parents are putting pressure on educational ad-
ministrators and governing boards to purchase and
use computers in all phases of education. We cannot
agree with W. L. Somervell, Jr., who contends that
the United States appears to be losing its high-
technology lead to other nations.[18] In support of our
optimistic view, we cite the popularity of microcomputers, the simplicity of skills needed to program
them, and the declining cost of hardware and software.
However, we do believe that there is inefficiency in
the way newly acquired knowledge is transferred to

those who would make use of it, for manipulating the
technology is simpler than learning the concepts of
planning models. For this reason, we have designed
this book so that the concepts are presented through
problems accompanied by appropriate software. The
microcomputer helps to make use of planning models,
research, policy studies, and assists in decision
making.

     Planners and decision makers do not have time to
study and conduct research in all the different areas
that complement the profession. For example, Judd[19]
acknowledged that the realities of time pressures on
educators have resulted in a strong interest in pre-
recorded computer programs. That is, if people have
good examples of computer programs and the methods
and models behind those programs, uses of microcomputer
programs and authorship of new or modified programs are
greatly facilitated. We have made a concerted effort
to present our material so that the creation of new or
modified computer programs is made easier for the
planner and decision maker. Spread sheet programs and
concepts are excluded since their role is in the area
of accounting. There are two positive outcomes that
can be expected from the concepts outlined in this
work and from microcomputers: (1) proper use of a
microcomputer can greatly improve the quality of information for decision making and planning, and
(2) operations within an organization will improve.[20]

     Presently there is an unprecedented wave of
development in microcomputer hardware and software.
The rapidly changing market competition is outlined
monthly in Educational Technology. During the past
two years most professional journals have devoted at
least one issue to what microcomputers can do for each
discipline. In education, Melmed[21] has perhaps cap-
tured the perception of the computer revolution by
stating that it is as important as the invention of
printing. Few will disagree with this statement. One
caution is in order: How will microcomputers affect
educational practice? It is suggested that microcomputers on their own are unlikely to promote any parti-
cular outcomes.[22]

SUMMARY

     Chapter 1 has provided an overview of some con-
cepts of planning endorsed by the authors of this
book. We have noted a variety of theories of planning
and suggested the rational-transactive theory as a
sound approach to planning and decision making. In
the last section some perceptions of the microcomputer
were presented. Background, the need for the microcomputer in planning, capabilities, and the rapidly
changing market were briefly discussed.

Chapter 2
Time Management
and Scheduling Methods

CONCEPTS OF TIME MANAGEMENT

One of our most valuable resources in planning is
time, yet managing it wisely continues to rank among
the most serious problems for individuals. Too frequently we are confronted with situations where lost
time means lost opportunities and lost money. Wasted
time, the enemy of the planner, has the tendency to
manage individuals and results in unachieved goals
and objectives. The outcome is a malfunctioning organization. In this chapter we will investigate time
management and scheduling in order to assist the planner and policy analyst in achieving goals and objectives on time.

The first step toward making time work for us,
according to Fox and Schwartz,[1] is to analyze how it
is used. Planning and scheduling time may be viewed
as a management technique at the individual (micro)
and at the organizational (macro) levels. Contrary to
what many reactive planners may say, we aren't "running
out" of time, but we can utilize time better through
scheduling and continuous assessment of how it is used.

Perhaps the best place to begin our analysis is
with a theory of time management. The theory that time
is money and that allocation of time parallels the allocation of money is indeed basic to individuals and
organizations. Thus, the primary step in time allocation at the micro level is to conduct an individual
needs assessment: "How productive am I now and how
productive should I be?" Perhaps one should parallel
this initial step with an analysis of the formal job
description and its comparison to a self-written job
description, since formal job descriptions often state
maximum required activities. This step must be completed before goal setting, for how can people know

how productive they could be if they don't know how
productive they are now. That is, one should have
knowledge of what exists, as well as of what is expected. Once the self-assessment task is started, and
it should be continuous, special attention may be given
to productivity for a specific time period. Cooper[2]
has dealt with the problem of how to accomplish tasks
in less time, and Drucker's work, <u>The Effective Execu-
tive</u>,[3] complements the time management concept by
focusing on improving effectiveness as a manager. Most
time management literature states that the lack of
goals, objectives, and priorities are chief characteristics of time wasters or time-wasting organizations.
Furthermore, the lack of self-discipline, organizational policy, and the inability to say "no" decreases
personal effectiveness.

Effectiveness of time management is a function of
knowing what the organization expects as well as understanding where one fits into the total organizational-
productivity framework. Thus, the organization must
be organized. One workable theoretical process for
organizing the organization is management by objectives
(MBO)[4] or a modified version of MBO, since the process
in its pure form is not totally amenable to public organizations. MBO is a process to increase productivity
by allowing systematic interaction among individuals
within the organization regarding goals, objectives,
and tasks. For example, each individual works coopera-
tively with superiors and subordinates in specifying
objectives and delineating when and how they will be
reached.[5] Perhaps the reason that MBO has not worked
well (especially the reward system has failed) is because of time wasters.

Specifying when a goal or objective is to be
achieved requires knowledge of the organization, an
understanding of how activities relate to each other,
and skill in time scheduling. Time management, according to Pryor,[6] is improved through activities such as
establishing priorities and scheduling one's time.
Time analysis of current individual practices precedes
embarking on a plan.[7] Furthermore, time analysis and
scheduling of project and organizational activities
are recommended before beginning a plan.

There are other issues relevant to time management
such as control of time wasters, attempting too much,
delegation of responsibility, and effective communica-
tions. This chapter deals with issues of this nature
and especially the process of efficiently scheduling
time in order to achieve goals and objectives. Organizational activities and the policy process are difficult to schedule, but this problem may be minimized
by using the time-scheduling procedures in the following sections.

SCHEDULING ACTIVITIES

First we shall investigate the time management
process by looking into some problems at the micro
level. Assume, for example, that you, a well-informed
individual, have the objective of getting to work by
8 A.M., but you experience great difficulty in getting
out of bed early enough to get dressed, eat breakfast
and drive to work. These activities require that you
rise at or before 6:25 A.M. Now the stage is set for
the first lesson in time management as presented in
Problem 2.1.

Problem 2.1.   Based on the above constraints and
the following ten activities that begin at 6:25 A.M.,
determine a schedule that will help meet your policy
objective of getting to your office at least by 8 A.M.
each morning.

Activity	Time (in Minutes)
A - Getting out of bed	5
B - Shower and shave	15
C - Watch or read the morning	
news and weather report	15
D - Select clothes	2
E - Get dressed	8
F - Prepare breakfast	12
G - Eat breakfast	15
H - Brush teeth	3
I - Listen to recorded lecture	
on time management	20
J - Drive to work	25
Total	120 minutes

Solution.   Since the starting time was 6:25 A.M.,
we note that by performing each activity in a linear
manner the time is 8:25 A.M. when the objective is
finally reached. By omitting the morning news and the
lecture, the goal may be reached; however, you wish to
be informed about current events and the recorded lec-
tures (on time management, policy planning, and other
job-related subjects) are also very important to your
job success and performance.

In this hypothetical situation a few modifications
can be made and some activities could be accomplished
in parallel in order to achieve the objective. Figure
2.1 illustrates a scheduling procedure appropriate for
an acceptable solution if Activity C is changed to
"listen to the morning news and weather" and Activity I
is accomplished while driving to work. That is, Activities B and C and Activities I and J are performed simultaneously (in parallel).

In Figure 2.1 note the circle, arrow, and dashed
arrow. The circle is called a node and represents the

Figure 2.1.   Network of Activities for Arriving at Work on Time
                (Problem 2.1)

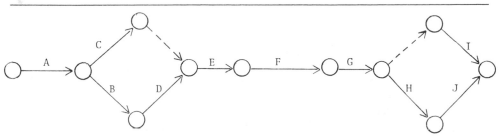

beginning and ending of an activity, which is indicated
by an arrow. Some of the literature on networking also
defines the node as an "event." The activity arrow
designates time, while the dashed arrow denotes that
no time has elapsed. The latter symbol is referred to
as a "dummy" activity and is used as a networking technique to "tie together" the various activities and may
or may not show dependence between certain activities.

    By summing the required times along the path A, B,
D, E, F, G, H, and J we find that the total time has
been reduced from 120 to 85 minutes. Thus, the arrival
time is 7:50 A.M.

    Now consider the modifications suggested in
Problem 2.2.

    Problem 2.2.   Construct a network for Problem 2.1
and find the path with the largest amount of time if
(1) Activity F is performed by someone else, (2) Activity C is "listen to the morning news and weather," and
(3) Activity I is accomplished while driving to work.

    Solution.   The network representing a solution to
this problem is shown in Figure 2.2. The path from the
beginning to the end of the network having the largest
amount of time is called the "critical path." In Figure 2.2 the total time along the critical path (A, B,
D, E, G, H, and J) is 73 minutes. Hence, the solution
has been improved from 120 to 73 minutes.

    Perhaps you are wondering why the dummy Activity D_1

Figure 2.2.   Network of Activities for Problem 2.2

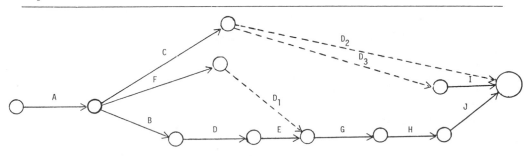

ties back into the network and why D_2 and D_3 emerge
after Activity C in Figure 2.2. First, consider parallel Activities C, F, and B and note the activity or
activities that are dependent upon their completion.
For example, G, eat breakfast, is dependent upon the
completion of F, fix breakfast. Thus, D_1 simply ties
the relationship together. Note that D_2 merges with
the network at the final node, since Activity C was to
be completed prior to beginning the day's work. Perhaps Activities C and G could be parallel. This would
not influence the final outcome, however. Since Activities I and J are parallel, it was simply convenient
to tie C and I together with D_3. Here dependence was
not really necessary. Hence, one of the most difficult problems in networking has emerged--showing dependent relationships. Note that D is shown as dependent upon B. But, this sequence could be reversed, and
the final result would remain the same. Therefore,
when using dummy activities and sequencing, it is wise
to know what the final objective is and to be flexible
in performing the activities required to obtain it.

SCHEDULING TIME WITH CPM

The purpose of the critical path method (CPM) is to
allow the planner to schedule activities whereby they
conform to appropriate job sequences and completion
time is minimized. Prior to the development of CPM,
Henry L. Gantt devised a management system similar to
CPM. This methodology was concerned with scheduling
production by sequencing activities horizontally such
that operation could be controlled.[8] In Figure 2.3
we find a Gantt Chart listing seven activities and
their scheduled time periods. Activity G, for example, begins at the sixth time period and is completed
in the eighth. The numbers in the circles may be used
in sequencing the activity network. The major purpose
of the Gantt Chart, developed during World War I, was
to compare production with the promised completion
date.[9]

CPM provides the planner with a visual description
of activity dependence and relationships as opposed
to the Gantt Chart, which reveals the relationships
among activities horizontally. The activity network
of the Gantt Chart is illustrated in Figure 2.4. One
reason for using the network instead of the chart is
to determine the slack time that is available within
the network. To calculate the available slack time,
the amount of time required on each path within the
network is summed and the difference between the
longest path and each alternative path at points of
merger is determined (see Problem 2.3). In Figure 2.4
there are three paths: A, D, and G; B, C, and G; and
B, E, F, and G.

Figure 2.3.   Gantt Chart   Figure 2.4.   Activity Network
                                                   of Gantt Chart

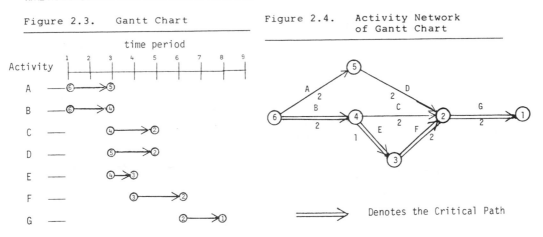

Problem 2.3.   Based on the information in Figures 2.3 and 2.4, find the critical path and points in the network where slack time is available.

Solution.   First we determine the critical path, when the time unit per activity is

$$A = 2, \qquad\qquad E = 1,$$
$$B = 2, \qquad\qquad F = 2,$$
$$C = 2, \qquad\qquad G = 2.$$
$$D = 2,$$

The following values result by summing the time units per path:

$$A + D + G = 6,$$
$$B + C + G = 6, \text{ and}$$
$$B + E + F + G = 7.$$

At node #2 we note that two alternate time paths merge with the critical path, which is B, E, F, G. Consequently, the time units at this point of merger are

$$A + D = 4,$$
$$B + C = 4, \text{ and}$$
$$B + E + F = 5.$$

Therefore, there is one unit of slack time available at node #2 for path A, D and one unit of slack for path B, C.

Determining slack time is important, especially if the critical path requires more time than is allotted for completion of the total set of activities. For example, if six time units were allotted to complete all the activities in the above problem, then the extra time units of slack could be applied to Activity F in order to adjust B, E, F, and G whereby any path would

require only six time units for completion. Eliminat-
ing the slack time could be achieved by hiring more
employees for Activity F or by allowing the staff to
work overtime to the point that all activities could
be completed within six time units. If there were no
possible way to utilize overtime, for this becomes ex-
pensive, or if no new employees could be hired because
of financial constraints, then there are at least three
alternatives left for the manager, assuming that six
time units were allotted and seven time units are required. One alternative is obvious--go beyond the allotted time. The second, although not good, would be
to quit, and the third alternative plan would be to re-
quest an additional time unit. Obviously, these are
the very problems that CPM is designed to solve before
any set of activities is started. That is, CPM allows
the planner to look into the future before attempting
to complete a set of activities or a project. Thus,
CPM is a planning methodology as well as a time management tool.

A MICROCOMPUTER SOLUTION TO THE CPM PROBLEM

       Figure 2.5 represents the same problem as shown in
Figure 2.4. In order to meet the constraints for the
CPM microcomputer program found in Appendix A, each

Figure 2.5.   Activity Network for Microcomputer
               Solution

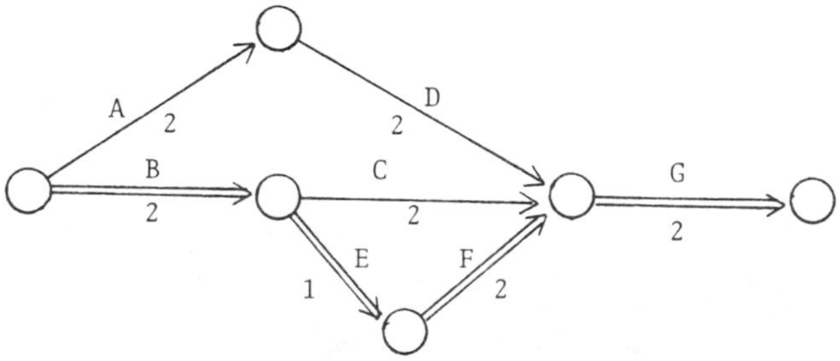

PATH	ACTIVITY Label	ACTIVITY Number	ACTIVITY Time
	A	1	2
ONE	D	3	2
	G	7	2
- -			
	B	2	2
TWO	C	4	2
	G	7	2
- -			
	B	2	2
THREE	E	5	1
	F	6	2
	G	7	2

path is numbered. For each path, the labeled activities are numbered and the appropriate completion times
are entered when the computer requests them.

Having stored the CPM microcomputer program, enter
"Run CPM." An example of the interactions required to
solve Problem 2.3 with the CPM microcomputer program
is shown below.

```
]RUN CPM
LABEL EACH ACTIVITY WITH A NUMBER

INPUT THE NUMBER OF ACTIVITIES ON THE ACTIVITY NETWORK.
?7

ENTER TIME FOR ACTIVITY 1
?2
ENTER TIME FOR ACTIVITY 2
?2
ENTER TIME FOR ACTIVITY 3
?2
ENTER TIME FOR ACTIVITY 4
?2
ENTER TIME FOR ACTIVITY 5
?1
ENTER TIME FOR ACTIVITY 6
?2
ENTER TIME FOR ACTIVITY 7
?2
Enter the number of paths: 3

Enter the number of activities which lie along path 1
?3

Enter the activities, by number, which lie along path 1
?1
?3
?7
Enter the number of activities which lie along path 2
?3

Enter the activities, by number, which lie along path 2
?2
?4
?7
Enter the number of activities which lie along path 3
?4

Enter the activities, by number, which lie along path 3
?2
?5
?6
?7
Path 3 is the critical path.

Length of critical path = 7
```

The student should have a working knowledge of CPM
prior to dealing with a problem "set-up" as presented
by the computer interaction system. A network should
be drawn and referenced in a manner similar to the
presentation in Figure 2.5. Because of these
constraints, we have provided a straightforward introduction to CPM and worked one problem completely before
involving the microcomputer in the solution of a
problem.

The CPM program is written in BASIC (Apple II), but there are only a few simple symbol changes necessary to make the program compatible among the various microcomputer systems. Problem 2.4 may be worked with the microcomputer and also serve as a foundation for more difficult problems. In this problem the term "major milestone" is introduced. In the context of this example, a major milestone is a goal to be achieved.

Problem 2.4.   The school board of a hypothetical school district makes a decision to construct a new facility. According to the major milestones and times (in days) presented below, determine the critical path for the construction project.

Activity	Completion Time (days)
A - Hire survey team	3
B - Forecast student enrollment	8
C - Survey program needs	30
D - Conduct community and economic analysis	26
E - Conduct facilities survey	29
F - Hire architect	10
G - Design educational specifications	30
H - Select site, develop facility blue-prints, and sell municipal bonds	35
I - Award construction contract	10
J - Construction	300

Solution.   There are four alternative paths from A to J shown in Figure 2.6. These paths and their expected times are

$$\text{Path} \quad I = A + B + C + D_1 + G + H + I + J = 416 \text{ days},$$
$$\text{Path} \quad II = A + B + E + D_2 + G + H + I + J = 415 \text{ days},$$
$$\text{Path} \quad III = A + D + F + D_2 + G + H + I + J = 414 \text{ days, and}$$
$$\text{Path} \quad IV = A + D + D_3 + I + J \qquad\qquad = 339 \text{ days}.$$

This is a very tight schedule, and with a delay of one day on Path II there would be two critical paths, but it is possible for all alternative paths in any network to be critical paths.

For most projects a subnetwork of activities is inherent. For example, consider Activity C (survey program needs). This major milestone will probably take much longer than 30 days, but for the sake of our example it might be broken out as shown in Table 2.1. Thus the subnetwork for Activity C (30 days) would be as shown in Figure 2.7. Consider the

Figure 2.6.   Construction Project Network

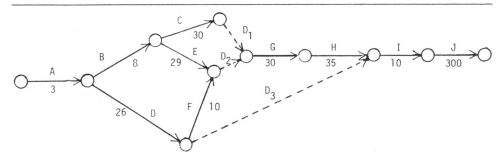

Table 2.1.   Problem 2.4, Activity C Broken Out

Activity	Time (days)
C_1 - Make specific assignments	2
C_2 - Survey needs for mathematics program	20
C_3 - Survey needs for English	20
C_4 - Survey needs for history	20
C_5 - Survey needs for vocational education	20
C_6 - Survey needs for special education	20
C_7 - Survey needs for arts	20
C_8 - Survey needs for sports	20
C_9 - Survey needs for finance	20
C_{10}- Write up needs assessment	5
C_{11}- Present findings to board	1
C_{12}- Revise and prepare final draft	2

Figure 2.7.   Activity C Subnetwork

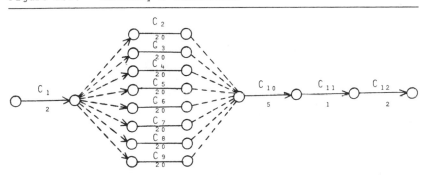

possibility that each of the original ten major milestones has subnetworks at least as complex as the one
for Activity C. Consequently, there is a good chance
that complications may develop and cause the need for
rescheduling. This possibility can be minimized if
the total project is well-organized and if the responsibilities for completing each activity are clearly
defined.

The technique of linear responsibility charting
(LRC) discussed by Hentschke[10] is an excellent approach to facilitating time management through organizing a project. LRC is a formal management device for delineating how people are organized and
how they should communicate. Thus, in Table 2.2 we
note, for example, that Activity C (survey program
needs) is the responsibility of the survey team, who
also does the work, while the board and superintendent must be consulted and informed.

TIME ANALYSIS WITH PERT

One important dimension of time management is completing a project within a specified time frame. For
example, in Problem 2.4 what if the board wants to
occupy the new facility within 390 work days from the
day the decision was made to start the construction

Table 2.2.   Linear Responsibility Table for Construction
             Project Network

Project Activity	Responsible Person(s)				
	Superintendent and Board	Survey Team	Architect	Business Manager	Contractor
A	I, II			II	
B	III	I, II			
C	III	I, II			
D	III	I, II			
E	III	I, II			
F	I, III			II, III	
G	III	I, II	III		
H	I, III	II	II	II	
I	I		III	II, III	
J	I, III	III	III	III	I, II

I - Responsible for the activity
II - Person(s) doing the work
III - Individual(s) that must be consulted and/or informed

project? This new problem would be appropriate for
analysis with the program evaluation and review technique (PERT). PERT is a time management method that
allows the planner to identify activities and estimate
the expected completion times associated with each
activity before beginning a project. PERT is different from CPM in that three time estimates are required
per activity. In PERT the required completion time
is compared with the expected completion time (critical
path), and a probability statement can be made relative
to meeting the required completion time. PERT, therefore, permits the planner to schedule project activities at appropriate times so that project costs are
conserved and completion time is expedited.[11]

In 1958 this widely known planning technique was
introduced collectively by the Navy Special Projects
Office, Booz, Allen, and Hamilton, and the Lockheed
Aircraft Corporation. Since then, this time management technique has been used continuously in business,
government, industry, agriculture, and education. Like
CPM, PERT is an outgrowth of work in scheduling and
planning initiated by Gantt.

Four objectives of PERT's methodology have been
described by the Department of the Navy as follows:

1. The fostering of increased orderliness and con-
    sistency in planning and evaluating. . . .
2. The providing of an automatic mechanism for the
    identification in all areas of potential trou-
    ble spots which arise as a result of a failure
    in one.
3. The structuring of a method to give operational
    flexibility to the program by allowing for ex-
    perimentation in a simulated sense.
4. The speedy handling and analysis of the inte-
    grated data, thus allowing for expeditious cor-
    rection of recognized trouble areas.[12]

According to the developers of PERT, "the basic approach of PERT is less novel than the execution of the
approach."[13] Its general objective is to provide a
periodic evaluation report to planners and administra-
tors. If a problem is emerging, as detected by network analysis, alternate courses of action are initiated. One basic factor to be considered by users
of the technique is that the system of evaluation of
events and time is based on human judgment. A second
qualification is that the PERT system can integrate
these judgments in an orderly, consistent, and rapid
manner--but quality of judgments is a constraint upon
the method. One very important characteristic of the
PERT system is that it should be a linking device between planners and decision makers. An early report
on the project summarized the basic approach of PERT
as follows:

1. Selection of specific, identifiable activi-
    ties which must occur along the way to suc-
    cessful conclusion of the project.
2. Sequencing of these activities and estab-
    lishing of interdependencies between them so
    that a project network is developed.
3. Estimate of time required to achieve these
    activities together with a measurement of the
    uncertainties involved.
4. Design of an analysis or evaluation proce-
    dure to process and manipulate these data.
5. Establishing of information channels to
    bring actual achievement data and change
    data to the evaluation point.
6. Application of electronic data processing
    equipment to the analysis procedure.[14]

Activity identification, critical to the completion
of a project, is the initial required step. When a
selection of activities has been completed, determina-
tion of their sequence and interdependence is the next
logical step toward network construction. A network
is constructed as a linked sequence of events connected
by activities necessary to achieve a given objective.
The PERT flow chart (network) represents identified
and sequential events according to their interrela-
tionships.

The third step involves estimating the time required per activity to accomplish the events and determining the uncertainties surrounding the completion of
the total project. Three different time estimates are
given for each activity arrow. Where possible, individuals who have had previous experience in the activity
should furnish the three time estimates. For example,
if a system flow chart is drawn to represent a curriculum development project, then three time estimates
to complete each activity should be made by experienced
curriculum planners. The three completion time estimates per activity are most optimistic (a); most
likely (m); and most pessimistic (b). The experienced
planner is asked to give the three estimates per activity in units such as hours, days, weeks, or months.

Assume that the three completion time estimates
for an activity A $\longrightarrow$ B are 2, 4, 6, respectively.
The equations developed to provide a single time estimate and variance for an activity are

$$t_e = \frac{a + 4m + b}{6} \text{ , and}$$

$$v^2 = \left(\frac{b - a}{6} \right)^2,$$

where t_e is the weighted time estimate and v^2 represents the variance for the activity. Substituting three time estimates into the above equation we find that

$$t_e = \frac{2 + 4(4) + 6}{6} ,$$

$$= \frac{24}{6} ,$$

$$= 4; \text{ and}$$

$$v^2 = \left[\frac{6 - 2}{6} \right]^2 ,$$

$$= .444....$$

Hence, the time required to complete activity A $\longrightarrow$ B is 4 units with a variance of .444. The square root of the variance gives the amount of negative or positive deviation for the expected time. Thus, $\sqrt{.444} = .666$, or the deviation (either negative or positive) for the 4 time units. In statistical terms, there is a 68 percent chance that the expected time, t_e, will be completed within 3.334 and 4.666 days $(4 - .666 = 3.334$ and $4 + .666 = 4.666)$.

In Figure 2.8 the belief of the time estimator(s) is demonstrated concerning the completion of the activity. The most optimistic time estimate (a) appears on

Figure 2.8. Probability That $t_e = 4$

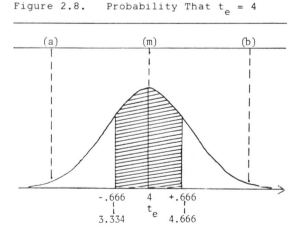

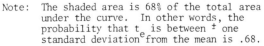

Note: The shaded area is 68% of the total area under the curve. In other words, the probability that t_e is between $\pm$ one standard deviation from the mean is .68.

the left side of the bell-shaped curve. At the peak
of the curve is shown the most likely time (m), and on
the right the most pessimistic time estimate (b) is
shown. Note that the activity time arrow moves from
left to right indicating increased time. The three
estimates are combined in order to formulate one estimate per activity. Small probabilities are associated
with the time estimates (a) and (b) in Figure 2.8. In
general, point (m) is free to take on any position between (a) and (b). This depends on the value judgment
of the estimators. Obtaining the three time estimates
per activity can be a complicated undertaking in a
large project. This job may become very difficult in
a project in which no one is familiar with the time
needed to complete certain activities. Frequently
these estimates become educated guesses; hence after
the project has been started, adjustments in time estimates may be necessary.

The application of PERT may be demonstrated with
Problem 2.5. In addition to the information presented in Problem 2.4, we shall use three time estimates and determine the probability of completing the
project, given a specific completion time.

Problem 2.5.   Determine the probability of completing the construction project outlined below within
425 work days.

	Completion Time (days)				
Major Milestone	a	m	b	t_e	v^2
A - Hire survey team	2	3	4	3	.111
B - Forecast student enrollment	6	8	10	8	.444
C - Survey program needs	25	30	35	30	2.778
D - Conduct community and economic analysis	8	10	12	10	.444
E - Conduct facilities survey	12	15	18	15	1.000
F - Hire architect	6	10	12	9.667	1.000
G - Design educational specifications	20	30	35	29.167	6.250
H - Select site, develop blue-prints, and sell bonds	30	35	45	35.833	6.250
I - Award construction contract	5	10	15	10	2.778
J - Construction	275	300	345	303.333	136.111

Solution.   Following the calculation of t_e and v^2
per activity we now determine the critical path from

the four alternative paths depicted in Figure 2.9:

Path   I = A + B + C + D$_1$ + G + H + I + J = 419.333 days,
Path II = A + B + E + D$_2$ + G + H + I + J = 404.333 days,
Path III = A + D + F + D$_2$ + G + H + I + J = 401 days, and
Path IV = A + D + D$_3$ + I + J   = 326.333 days.

Since Path I requires the greatest amount of time, we
now sum the variance (V^2) along the critical path in
order to determine the probability of completing the
project in 425 days. Thus, the variance along the
critical path is 154.722.

In order to determine the probability of completing the project in 425 days the equation for the
normal deviation (z score) is used. Specifically,

$$\frac{x}{\sigma} = \frac{\bar{x}_1 - \bar{x}_2}{\sigma} = z$$

is modified for the PERT problem, where $x_1 = T_L$ (time
allowed for project completion), $\bar{x}_2 = T_E$ (critical
path time), and $\sigma = \sqrt{\Sigma V^2}$ or the square root of the
sum of the variances of the activities on the criti-
cal path. Therefore,

$$z = \frac{T_L - T_E}{\sqrt{\Sigma V^2}}.$$

By substituting for each variable we find that

$$z = \frac{425 - 419.333}{\sqrt{154.722}},$$

Figure 2.9.   PERT Network of Construction Project

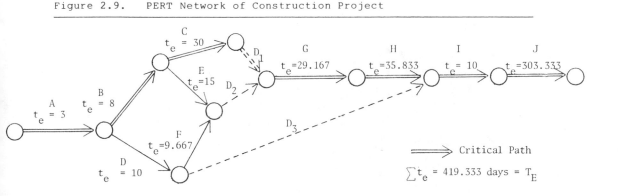

$$= \frac{5.667}{12.439} \,,$$

$$= .456 \,,$$

$$= .46.$$

By consulting Table 2.3 we find that the probability for $z = .4$ is .6554 and when $z = .5$ the probability is .6915. Interpolating as follows: $(.6915 - .6554) (.60) = .0217$, and summing .6554 and

Table 2.3.   Probability Distribution for PERT Problems

z	Area (Probability)	z	Area (Probability)
-3.0	.0013	3.0	.9987
-2.9	.0019	2.9	.9981
-2.8	.0026	2.8	.9974
-2.7	.0035	2.7	.9965
-2.6	.0047	2.6	.9953
-2.5	.0062	2.5	.9938
-2.4	.0082	2.4	.9918
-2.3	.0107	2.3	.9893
-2.2	.0139	2.2	.9861
-2.1	.0179	2.1	.9821
-2.0	.0228	2.0	.9772
-1.9	.0287	1.9	.9713
-1.8	.0359	1.8	.9641
-1.7	.0446	1.7	.9554
-1.6	.0548	1.6	.9452
-1.5	.0668	1.5	.9332
-1.4	.0808	1.4	.9192
-1.3	.0968	1.3	.9032
-1.2	.1151	1.2	.8849
-1.1	.1357	1.1	.8643
-1.0	.1587	1.0	.8413
-0.9	.1841	0.9	.8159
-0.8	.2119	0.8	.7881
-0.7	.2420	0.7	.7580
-0.6	.2743	0.6	.7257
-0.5	.3085	0.5	.6915
-0.4	.3446	0.4	.6554
-0.3	.3821	0.3	.6179
-0.2	.4207	0.2	.5793
-0.1	.4602	0.1	.5398
0.0	.5000	0.0	.5000

.0217, we have .6771. Thus the probability of completing the project within 425 days is P (z = .46) = .6771, or there is a 67.71 percent chance of meeting the expected completion time.

THE MICROCOMPUTER AND PERT

A considerable amount of the planner's time may be consumed in working a PERT problem without the aid of a computer. Furthermore, there are numerous places where errors may be made in calculations. The microcomputer program PERT is designed to save time, minimize errors, and provide a basis for the simulation of alternative solutions to various time management problems. The PERT program as shown in Appendix A may be expanded for larger problems and microcomputer systems with large amounts of storage.

Problem 2.5 illustrated the calculations of t_e, v^2, the critical path, and z--all of which require a great deal of time. We shall now apply the PERT program and obtain a solution to Problem 2.5.

To design a "setup" for the microcomputer application and solution, we must refer to Figure 2.9 and Problem 2.5 to generate the information in Table 2.4. Path I includes activities 1, 2, 3, 11, 7, 8, 9, and 10. Path II includes activities 1, 2, 5, 12, 7, 8, 9, and 10. Path III contains activities 1, 4, 6, 12, 7, 8, 9, and 10. Path IV involves activities 1, 4, 13, 9, and 10.

Table 2.4.   Setup for Microcomputer Application for PERT

Activity	Activity Number	Activity Times
A	1	2- 3- 4
B	2	6- 8-10
C	3	25-30-35
D	4	8-10-12
E	5	12-15-18
F	6	6-10-12
G	7	20-30-35
H	8	30-35-45
I	9	5-10-15
J	10	275-300-345
D_1	11	0- 0- 0
D_2	12	0- 0- 0
D_3	13	0- 0- 0

The interactions below illustrate how the problem
is solved with the microcomputer. The return key is
pressed after each entry.

```
]RUN PERT
After labeling each activity on the PERT
Chart with a number, label each with
the most optimistic, the most likely,
and the most pessimistic time for
completion.

INPUT THE NUMBER OF ACTIVITIES ON THE   PERT CHART.
?13
Beginning with ACTIVITY 1 and continuing
in numerical order, enter first the most
optimistic, then the most likely, and
finally the most pessimistic time for
completion for each activity.

ENTER TIMES FOR ACTIVITY 1
?2
?3
?4
ENTER TIMES FOR ACTIVITY 2
?6
?8
?10
ENTER TIMES FOR ACTIVITY 3
?25
?30
?35
ENTER TIMES FOR ACTIVITY 4
?8
?10
?12
ENTER TIMES FOR ACTIVITY 5
?12
?15
?18
ENTER TIMES FOR ACTIVITY 6
?6
?10
?12
ENTER TIMES FOR ACTIVITY 7
?20
?30
?35
ENTER TIMES FOR ACTIVITY 8
?30
?35
?45
ENTER TIMES FOR ACTIVITY 9
?5
?10
?15
ENTER TIMES FOR ACTIVITY 10
?275
?300
?345
ENTER TIMES FOR ACTIVITY 11
?0
?0
?0
ENTER TIMES FOR ACTIVITY 12
?0
?0
?0
ENTER TIMES FOR ACTIVITY 13
?0
?0
```

```
?0
Input the number of paths: 4

Enter the number of activities which lie on path 1
?8

Enter the activities, by number, which lie along path 1
?1
?2
?3
?11
?7
?8
?9
?10
Enter the number of activities which lie on path 2
?8

Enter the activities, by number, which lie along path 2
?1
?2
?5
?12
?7
?8
?9
?10
Enter the number of activities which lie on path 3
?8

Enter the activities, by number, which lie along path 3
?1
?4
?6
?12
?7
?8
?9
?10
Enter the number of activities which lie on path 4
?5

Enter the activities, by number, which lie along path 4
?1
?4
?13
?9
?10
ENTER TIME ALLOWED FOR COMPLETION OF THE PROJECT.
?425
Path 1 is the critical path.



WEIGHTED TIME ESTIMATE = 419.333333


Z FOR COMPLETION IN 425 UNITS OF TIME = .479873818

]
```

The following problem provides an expanded perspective of PERT.

Problem 2.6. Assume that we have the same set of constraints as outlined in Problem 2.5. What is the probability of completing the project within 420 days?

Solution.   By substituting the appropriate data
in the formula

$$z = \frac{T_L - T_E}{\sqrt{\Sigma V^2}} \, ,$$

we find that

$$z = \frac{420 - 419.333}{\sqrt{154.722}} \, ,$$

$$= \frac{.677}{12.439} \, ,$$

$$= .054,$$

$$= .05.$$

Therefore the probability of completing the project
within 420 days is P (z = .05) = .5199.

In either of the two preceding problems there is
not any cause to be alarmed regarding meeting the expected completion date. However, a 50/50 chance is
not as desirable as say a 75 percent chance. Obviously
the planner should watch the situation presented in
Problem 2.6, since any minor malfunction at any point
in the project would mean a time overrun and perhaps
additional cost.

SUMMARY

The problem of time management has been discussed
in terms of scheduling activities. In the first section of the chapter special attention has been given
to examples of time management at the micro (individual)
level, while the latter sections focus on time management at the organizational level. Time scheduling has
been approached through the utilization of CPM and
PERT, and these techniques are introduced through
practical problems. Presentation of these two
popular time-scheduling techniques begins with a
very simple problem, and each of the five subsequent problems introduces additional features of the
two techniques. For example, Problem 2.4 ties the
activities of a project to a linear responsibility
chart.
In Appendix B are five additional problems (with
answers) designed to provide the reader with a solid

foundation in time scheduling. Now that the basic
foundations for PERT and CPM have been completed, it
is suggested that the reader take the time to work
these problems using the microcomputer programs that
are found in Appendix A.

Chapter 3
Methods
of Community, Regional,
and Economic Analyses

The purpose of this chapter is to present some
important considerations concerning demographic,
social, and economic variables of a community or
region that should be analyzed when planning policies, programs, and facilities. Special emphasis is
placed on technique of analysis and how future trends
may be deduced.

The following questions are important for our
discussion: What are the important community and
regional characteristics that affect the educational
policies and programs serving a given population?
How do relationships among selected variables influence the policies of the total educational environment? These questions guide our attention to major
variables such as philosophy, policies, population,
and the economy of a community or region. Many components of these variable categories often have a
cause and effect relationship on the total community
environment. For example, when the mean education
level increases in a region or community, the per
capita income is also expected to increase. Furthermore, persons in a high socioeconomic community are
more likely to support tax increases for public service than those living in a less-educated and low-
income community.[1]

HISTORICAL TRENDS AND COMMUNITY ATTITUDES

A brief historical analysis of the community is
always an important document for the planner to
develop. Although written statements of purpose may
not exist, the analyst, through historical investigation, will discover the community's general philosophy of education as well as some significant

policies that have guided public service developments
and trends. The planner should keep in mind these
questions: Has the community supported public services adequately through bond issues and taxes? What
are the past and present attitudes of the community
concerning public services?

Perhaps selected reviews of the minutes of public
meetings will reveal the community's philosophy toward
the support of public services. Frequently governing
policies are revealed through the study of minutes of
public meetings and published handbooks. The reviews
of legislation and newspaper reports over several
years also provide information pertaining to policy,
philosophy, and general attitude trends. With regard
to certain agencies, it is important for the planner-
analyst to investigate the formal organizational
changes over several years for the purpose of outlining
trends relative to programs and governance. For example, with respect to education, What is the history of
the school board concerning approving budgets? What
are the trends regarding size of the board? What are
the local trends concerning elected or appointed boards
and superintendents?

A mathematical history of population characteristics is a vital data set for the planner to compile in
order to compare changes in growth over the past 20 or
30 years. Another key variable to be investigated is
the educational characteristics of the total population. The planner must know the answer to questions
such as, How does the expenditure per pupil compare
with state, regional, and national statistics on expenditures? What are the trends in employment and
housing?

To complement the historical trends, the planner
should assess the current attitudes of the community
on any matter related to a given issue. For example,
the researcher may develop some simple, straightforward questions designed to assess the attitude of
the public concerning the issue of financing education.
Obviously the planner should take every precaution to
construct a clear, concise interview format and instrument to be administered to a representative sample of
the population. There are several sources that will
facilitate this task. For example, Hyman[2] has developed
a significant, and now classic, work dealing with the
principles, cases, and procedures of survey design and
analysis. Methods, procedures, and techniques of analyses, as well as ways to reduce the cost of surveys
have been published by Sudman,[3] while Kerlinger[4] has
focused on research design, reliability, analysis,
methods of data collection, and proper ways to conduct
interviews. Perhaps one of the most popular references
for survey analysis, which also includes historical
methodology, has been written by Good.[5]

Population characteristics acquire a broader meaning for the planner when accompanied by a brief history
of industrial and business growth. Frequently, the
planner-analyst fails to consider the important fact
that education is also a business, since within many
communities the employees in education receive the
single largest payroll when compared to other businesses or industries. Hence, the economy of the
total community is influenced by education and
education-related businesses and industries.

The following section emphasizes the most significant aspects of population characteristics.
Certain components of the planning document, such as
a mathematical history of the total population, may
overlap with the historical section without being
woefully redundant.

THE POPULATION: PAST, PRESENT, AND FUTURE

Primary data sources for population analysis are
the U.S. Census and the local and regional planning
agencies. The planner should use the data from these
sources to make new forecasts or adjust those that
are outdated. Information from local utility companies, housing agencies, and telephone companies are
generally reliable and need little modification.
Perhaps forecasts provided by chambers of commerce
should be used as a guideline, but the planner should
be cautious here since their trends are frequently
too optimistic. To illustrate the process of data
collection and analysis more specifically, we shall
develop the main hard data components needed in a
planning document.

Assume that we are interested in assessing the
population growth of a selected county, County A, for
the purpose of our illustration. We should begin by
obtaining a recent map from the state highway department. If County A is adjacent to another state, we
would also obtain population information, economic
data, and maps from the adjacent state. All adjacent
counties, in or out of state, should be given consideration, since there is always an exchange of com-
muters and economic impacts cross state lines. We
shall conduct a hypothetical analysis of the populations of County A and the four bordering counties
(B, C, D, and E). Eventually we want to know how
many school-aged students are expected over the next
30 years, since our major goal is to plan for adequate
facilities that will house the public educational
program.

The historical population trends of the hypothetical five-county area are shown in Table 3.1.
Our job is to determine the future trend for the

Table 3.1. Historical Population Trends of Counties A, B, C, D, and E

Population

County	Census 30 Years Prior	Census 20 Years Prior	Rate of Change	Census 10 Years Prior	Rate of Change	Most* Recent Census	Rate of Change
A	28,892	24,700	-.1446	26,420	.0696	31,479	.1915
B	16,054	13,462	-.1615	15,826	.1756	17,228	.0886
C	20,828	31,066	.4915	32,149	.0349	35,409	.1014
D	18,674	15,286	-.1814	16,738	.0950	19,271	.1513
E	30,608	25,987	-.4621	26,890	.0347	31,750	.1807
Total	115,056	110,501		118,023		135,137	

*Most recent census or most recent estimate from a reliable source such as the state planning agency.

total population. One way to do this is by establishing the rate of change over several years. To determine the rate of change, we divide the difference of
two consecutive data bases by the least recent amount.
For example, the rate of change (-.1446) for County A
is determined as follows: [(24,700 - 28,892 = -4,192)
÷ 28,982 =]-.1446.

Our next step in the population analysis is to
look at those variables directly related to the economy. Hence, we shall investigate the trends in the
number of available jobs, the labor force, and the number of households within the five-county area (See
Table 3.2). These major economic indicators provide a
sound base from which to forecast the total population.
There are several different approaches to forecasting
economic variables. Most frequently the minimum,
average, and maximum categories are provided per forecast on variables such as birth rates, emigration,
immigration, death rates, number of available jobs,
and households. Our examples shall use only the average forecast, but maximum and minimum ranges are recommended when studying economic indicators. The examples
here are predicated on the hypothesis that migration
depends upon the economy, which we shall assume will
gradually improve.

If we are to forecast the total population of
County A, the two variables that need careful consideration are households within County A and the total
number of jobs in the five-county area. Population
shifts are related to the number of available jobs,[6]
and it is obvious that people must have available
housing. Consequently, we shall depend upon the relationships of jobs and housing in our example of forecasting population. Because the number of jobs is
dependent on the economy, let us assume a gradual increase in jobs over the next 30 years as generated in
the simple and straightforward calculations shown
below. These data are taken from Table 3.2.

Year	Number of Jobs	Rate of Change
30 years ago	40,656	
20 years ago	39,046	-.039600551
10 years ago	41,704	+.0680735543
Present	47,752	+.14502206

The algebraic sum of the rates of change is +.173495064,
and the average rate is +.0578316879. The present number of jobs (47,752) for the five-county area is now
substituted into the standard compound interest (SCI)
formula 47,752 $(1 + rate)^t$, where rate is .0578316879
and t=1, 10 years from now; t=2, 20 years from now; and
t=3, 30 years from now. Therefore, the number of jobs
expected for planning years 10, 20, and 30 is calculated as shown:

Table 3.2.   Major Economic Indicators for County A and the Totals for Counties A, B, C, D, and E

	Census 30 Years Ago		Census 20 Years Ago		Census 10 Years Ago		Most Recent Census	
	County A	Total	County A	Total	County A	Total	County A	Total
Population	28,892	115,056	24,700	110,501	26,420	118,023	31,479	135,137
Households	9,029	33,840	7,719	32,500	8,256	34,713	9,837	39,746
Labor Force *	16,605	65,373	14,195	62,784	15,184	67,058	18,091	76,782
Number of Jobs	10,281	40,656	8,790	39,046	9,402	41,704	11,202	47,752

*Total population 15-64 years of age.   (Source: U.S. Census)

$$PY10 = 47752 \ (1+.0578316879)^1,$$
$$= 47752 \ (1.0578316879)^1,$$
$$= 50514.$$
$$PY20 = 47752 \ (1.0578316879)^2,$$
$$= 53435.$$
$$PY30 = 47752 \ (1.0578316879)^3,$$
$$= 56525$$

Forecasting according to this procedure depends upon the basic assumption that the rate of growth over the next 30 years will be the same as the average of the historical data set. Sometimes we find that planning is based on this procedure alone, but one should be aware of the limitations under this assumption.

THE MICROCOMPUTER AND SCI

Since saving time is of primary concern to the planner, not to mention accuracy in calculations, we have provided a curve linear model programmed for the microcomputer (see Stand Compound Interest Model in Appendix A). The SCI allows for an easy method of forecasting if a constant rate of change is expected.

Using the data above, select "Stand Compound Interest Model" in Appendix A. Interactions that parallel the job-forecasting calculations detailed above are shown in the following example. After each "?" enter the data.

```
]RUN
NUMBER OF TIME PERIODS FOR WHICH DATA   ARE AVAILABLE:
?3
 LENGTH OF TIME PERIOD IN YEARS:
?10
BEGINNING WITH OLDEST DATA, ENTER DATA  CONSECUTIVELY:
?40656
?39046
?41704
?47752


PY10     50514
PY20     53435
PY30     56525
PY40     59794
```

An expansion of above concept is found in Problem 3.1.

Problem 3.1. Forecast the expected number of households in County A for PY10, PY20, and PY30 based on the results of the above example and the data shown in Table 3.2.

Solution. Our first task here is to establish the relationship between total number of jobs and households, as shown below.

Year	Households in County A	Total Number of Jobs in the Five Counties	Percentage
-30	9,029	40,656	22.21
-20	7,719	39,046	19.77
-10	8,256	41,704	19.80
Present	9,837	47,752	20.60
		Total	82.38
		Average	20.60

By taking the product of the average percent and the previously forecasted total number of jobs per planning interval, we arrive at the expected number of households as calculated below:

Year	Expected Number of Jobs		Average		Households in County A
PY10	50,514	x	.2060	=	10,406
PY20	53,435	x	.2060	=	11,008
PY30	56,525	x	.2060	=	11,644

Again this forecast is linear and directly dependent upon the assumptions underlying the forecast for the expected number of jobs. Obviously the relationship between jobs and households is assumed. Since the analysis entails the total number of jobs within the five-county area, the relationship is perhaps more acceptable than if we had not determined the total jobs for the surrounding counties. Remember County A is located in the center of the total group of five counties. The important variable of commuting to jobs across county lines is minimized if we also assume available housing and acceptable living conditions within County A. Results generated here facilitate the solution to Problem 3.2.

Problem 3.2. Forecast the population of County A for PY10, PY20, and PY30 from the percentage relationships between population and total jobs in Table 3.2 and the estimated number of total jobs for the five-county area calculated above.

Solution. Using data from Table 3.2 the following percentages are obtained:

Year	Population of County A	Total Jobs	Percentage
-30	28,892	40,656	71.06
-20	24,700	39,046	63.26
-10	26,420	41,704	63.35
Present	31,479	47,752	65.92
		Total	263.59
		Average	65.90

The relationship between the population in County A
and total number of jobs over the four data intervals is 65.90 percent. Consequently, 65.90 percent
times the total number of jobs in the five-county area
per planning interval results in the population estimate. Specifically,

$$PY10 = (.6590) (50,514),$$
$$33,289, \text{ the population of County A in PY10.}$$
$$PY20 = (.6590) (53,435),$$
$$= 35,214.$$
$$PY30 = (.6590) (56,525),$$
$$= 37,250.$$

There is one very important characteristic of this
analysis that is worth stressing--the fact that consideration was given to the total five-county area.
That is, the planner has developed a forecast of
population for one county that is dependent on the
total number of expected jobs (an economic variable)
in the total five-county area. This relationship is
not affected as long as the unemployment rate does
not rise significantly. However, there are other
models to consider, if our above assumptions are
seriously questioned. For example, the neoclassical
model[7] analyzes the growth of capital and labor with
respect to population changes. The labor surplus
economy model,[8] another alternative approach, focuses
on the assumption that a person may hold more than
one job. The latter model would mean that we can assume the total number of jobs is not necessarily
directly related to the size of the population.

FAMILY AND HOUSEHOLD CHARACTERISTICS

In order to forecast accurately the total population and the expected population densities, the planner should pay special attention to the population per
household and the physical conditions of the housing.
Our data in Table 3.2 reveal 3.2 individuals per household unit in County A (28,892 ÷ 9,029 = 3.199). We
therefore need to know how many housing units are needed
to accommodate the expected population for PY10, PY20,
and PY30. Most frequently the housing characteristics
are outlined by the U.S. Census as sound, deteriorat-
ing, and dilapidated. Frequently we find that an average of about 10 to 15 percent of the households are
categorized as dilapidated. Thus, if the population
forecast is accurate, new housing units must be constructed. Otherwise, we can expect the population to
shift to available housing and commute to the available
jobs. As an illustration, let us consider our household forecast for County A from Problem 3.1. Our data
reveal:

Year	Number of Households	Change
Present	9,837	
PY10	10,406	569
PY20	11,008	602
PY30	11,644	636

This straightforward calculation reveals a need for
1807 new housing units over the next 30 years, but if
we assume 10 percent of the existing homes are classi-
fied as dilapidated, each planning interval should be
increased at least by 10 percent to ensure available
housing. Hence, the present households (9,837) times
.10 = 984, the needed replacement of dilapidated homes
between the present and PY10. This process is continued for PY20 and PY30 in the solution to Problem
3.3. By knowing the expected number of new homes, the
researcher also has valuable information concerning
the new tax base for supporting public services.

Problem 3.3.   Determine the expected need for new
housing units for County A over the next 30 years.
Assume a 10 percent rate of dilapidation and a 30-year
lifetime for an average house.

Solution.   The number of housing units needed may
be calculated according to the following steps.

Step 1:   (9,837) (present housing units) times .10
= 984, the number of units needed over the
next 10 years (PY10) as a result of dilapidation.

Step 2:   (9,837 - 984) = 8,853, and 8,853 (.10) =
885, the number of units needed from PY10 to
PY20.

Step 3:   (8,853 - 885) = 7,968 and 7,968 (.10) =
797, the number of units needed from PY20 to
PY30.

By adding the change in the number of expected units
needed as a result of population increase and the number of units needed as a result of blight and dilapidation, we calculate the actual new required units:

PY10	569	+	984	=	1553.
PY20	602	+	885	=	1487.
PY30	636	+	797	=	1433.

These estimates may appear to be large at first, but
when expressed on a yearly basis we note that approximately 149 new housing units per year are required to
keep pace with the expected growth. Obviously there
will be a range in quality, and many of these units
will be mobile. Furthermore, the cost of money to
finance housing will be a significant factor influen-
cing population density.

Other characteristics of the population, such as

percentage white and non-white, should be incorporated
into our planning methods through charts, graphs, and
long range forecasts of their expected impacts on
housing, jobs, and the economy.

THE MICROCOMPUTER SOLUTION FOR DETERMINING
NEW HOUSING UNITS

   In determining the expected need for new housing
units to serve a given population, the variable "rate
of dilapidation" may range from .05 to .15 per hundred
over a ten-year period. This variable may be easily
changed in the microcomputer program to meet regional
differences. One reason that the planner needs to
know the expected new housing units is to estimate
revenue for property tax. The model covers 30 years
or the length of time just short of adding new homes
to the dilapidation group. Problem 3.3 may be solved
by entering the command, "Run New Housing Units."
The interactions that result follow:

```
RUN NEW HOUSING UNITS
Enter the number of time periods for
which forecasts of the number of
households are available:
?3

Enter the length of the time periods:
?10
Enter the rate of dilapidation:
?.10
Enter the number of households at
present:
?9837


Beginning with PY10, enter forecasts
of households:
?10406
?11008
?11644
PLANNING YEAR        NEW UNITS REQUIRED
     PY10                1552.7
     PY20                1487.33
     PY30                1432.797
```

   Since we have developed the population forecast
around available jobs, our forecast for housing might
need refinement, especially since we have assumed 3.2
persons per household. If we expect 2.75 persons per
household over the next 30 years instead of 3.2, then
the number of housing units should be increased. Lower
yield per household is always expected in high socio-
economic areas. However, there is always a need for
the planner to provide minimum, average, and maximum
forecasts per planning interval whereby other segments
of the economy may react in time to meet the expected
goals.

EDUCATION, AGE, SEX, AND RACE OF THE POPULATION

A mathematical history of the number of years of school completed and a profile of the age, sex, and race statistics for the community are important in assessing an area's ability to attract business and industry. County A must maintain a level of education equal to or better than the state level if it is going to be attractive for potential industrial and business growth. The level of education for the population 25 years old and over is usually the basis for comparison. As an example, consider the educational data for persons 25 years old and over in the five-county area, County A, and the state as shown in Table 3.3. From these data we can conclude that County A has a better chance of attracting business and industry that provide higher paying jobs than the five-county area or the state. Further analysis of education level by sex and race will also reveal important findings for expected business and industrial growth.

Another significant comparison concerns the distribution of the work force by age, sex, and race. One useful presentation of data is in the form of a profile or bar chart according to work force by these parameters. In a display of this nature the planner may note, for example, that the work force of males ages 35 through 39 is expected to double by PY30, yet a small increase is expected in the female population by PY30. To expand the example, assume that the non-white classification ages 35 through 39 reveals a marked difference for PY30 when compared to the white work force for the same age classification. Numerous comparisons of this nature may be made. It is important that they be tied to education since we know that a higher education level implies a higher rate of support for education through taxation. Comparisons of total personal income for a county, an area, and the state also are important for planning future educational support.

Table 3.3.   Educational Data for Persons 25 Years and Older

| Years of School | Percentages | | |
Completed	County A	Area	State
0 - 4	16.30	23.83	29.06
5 - 8	33.00	32.88	35.04
9 - 12	38.90	32.13	27.04
13+	11.80	11.16	8.86
Median	9.1	7.9	7.5

OTHER SIGNIFICANT ECONOMIC INDICATORS

Previously we noted that the major economic indicators centered around employment or the number of
available jobs in the hypothetical five-county area
of our analysis. When the planner develops a total
study according to the outline in this chapter, it
will be clear that the two major sources of data are
the U.S. Census and the State Economic Abstract.
Other planning agencies also provide data sources
and their own forecasts, but before these analyses
and forecasts are used in a planning document, it is
perhaps wise to determine how the various forecasts
were actually made. The planner should be especially
interested in the allowances for error in these
forecasts.

The importance of comparative analysis in developing a planning document cannot be overemphasized.
Hence, in this chapter frequent comparisons between
County A and the area, between County A and the state,
and between the area and the state are provided as
examples. The planning document should focus on comparisons within the general geographic region because
of distinct state laws that govern taxation of business and industry. Frequently, adjacent states have
significantly different attitudes toward taxing industries. For example, a set of taxes focusing on
corporate profits or income in one state may be much
more liberal in an adjacent state. This may also
occur to some degree among adjacent counties within a
state, and within one county a certain city may im-
pose different tax structures. To give a broad perspective on the structure of taxes, Johns and Morphet[9]
have provided a good discussion on taxation as sources
of revenue. Benson[10] also gives a thorough presentation of the nature of local, state, and federal taxation that is helpful in understanding the various tax
structures. Next, for the purpose of guiding the
planner through a useful analysis, we shall review
some additional variables that reveal the economic
foundation of an area.

THE ECONOMIC BASE OF A COMMUNITY

If the planner is to plot the future growth of a
certain community, the number of available jobs is a
necessary but not totally adequate data base. We must
also study the income that these jobs provide for the
community and the area. Therefore, a sound data base
for assessing the economy includes the number of jobs
and total personal income. Personal income is the
amount of money per person within a given area, less

such items as corporate profits, social insurance, and corporate profits tax, plus government payments to persons, less personal tax payments. Table 3.4 describes the personal disposable income for our hypothetical five-county area. We note that County A's percentage of state income has shown a decrease of .0053 over the past 30 years, while its percentage of the area income has slightly increased.

The amount of payroll taxes available for support of public services would also be needed in the planning document. Perhaps further comparison between the state and its neighbors and between the state and national personal income would also be appropriate for the planning document especially in developing forecasts. For example, if the state percentage decreases when compared to the national income, we could conclude that our area of study has not been keeping pace with the national economy to the point that a local depression has been experienced. Hence, the forecast should recognize the slow pace of overcoming the depressed economic conditions.

The contribution to the economy by agriculture is included in the personal disposable income. If the area of study relies heavily on agriculture, the planner should emphasize this fact. A table should be developed to illustrate an appropriate comparison of the mean value of farms. This will enable the planner to study property values for the purpose of taxation. It also gives a perspective on land use, since land use influences student population density. A similar table for the value of homes, value of business and industry, as well as an analysis of total land use is also suggested whereby a total picture of property values may be viewed. If the community contains a large amount of government-owned property

Table 3.4. Total Personal Disposable Income: State, Area, and County A[*]

	20 Years Ago	10 Years Ago	Present
State	$10,756,000	$17,748,000	$22,600,000
Area	577,882	582,224	619,200
County A	156,664	182,232	209,424
% of State	.0146	.0103	.0093
% of Area	.2711	.3130	.3382

*Dollars in thousands

(state and federal), we may find higher property taxes
to support public services. Property taxes frequently
correlate positively with economic progress.

Retail trade as an index of economic activity is
shown in Table 3.5. Here we note that County A is in
relatively good position when compared to the area.
Later in the analysis we will need to know how much
local sales tax is collected in County A. Therefore,
column five of Table 3.5 reveals the current sales tax
collection. This 2% sales tax generated a total of
$1,018,280 for the support of public services provided
by the county. By establishing a trend for several
planning years, we will be able to determine the expected level of support to be generated through sales
taxes. Tables such as Table 3.5 should be developed
for at least the past five years to facilitate further
comparisons with state, regional, and national statistics. An analysis of this nature would also provide
an excellent indicator of business activities. With
respect to data as shown in Table 3.5, we should consider the geographic location of County A. Major air,
land, and water routes, as well as climate, might be
significant factors to explain the success of County A
as compared to the total area. If much of the area
were mountainous and County A were in a valley, for
example, these variables would become significant in
the explanation of County A's success.

The success of hypothetical County A is revealed in
wholesale trade and service as described in Table 3.6.
Average sales of County A are ahead of the area. If
a more detailed comparison is desired for the planning
document, the planner might further compare wholesale
trade with the state and region as an assessment of
economic activities. Data on service establishments
are also presented in Table 3.6. Taxes on payroll,
sales, and receipts are given for the purpose of determining the amount of revenue available for public services. From tax revenues, such as outlined here, the
planner will be able to establish trends from historical data, relate these trends to expected economic activities, and forecast future revenues. The service
industry of County A leads the area in receipts, establishing our study area as a leading trade center. To
complement wholesale and retail trade, bank deposits,
presented in tabular form, may also be used as a measure of economic activities. Time and demand deposits
tend to show how the labor force reacts to recession
or increased economic activities.

A profile of occupation is important when developing a community analysis for the purpose of determining
what public services a population will demand and support. For example, we can expect a highly skilled
population to be more supportive of public services

Table 3.5. Retail Trade and Sales Tax Collected for County A and Retail Trade for the Area over the Past Fiscal Year

Business	County A				Area		
	No.	Total Sales*	Average Sales*	Sales Tax Collected in County A	No.	Total Sales*	Average Sales*
Total Retail	283	29,357	103.7	587,140	1,059	77,940	73.6
Lumber, Hdw.,etc.	15	2,121	141.4	42,420	48	5,988	124.8
Gen. Mdse.	20	1,155	57.8	23,100	88	6,478	73.6
Food Stores	93	6,646	71.5	132,920	370	21,152	57.2
Auto Dealers	15	3,732	248.8	74,640	109	15,386	141.9
Service Stations	28	1,844	65.9	36,880	129	7,786	60.4
Apparel	21	1,484	70.7	29,680	72	4,472	62.1
Furniture, Home Furnishings	11	558	50.7	11,160	50	2,389	47.8
Eating & Drinking	14	526	37.6	10,520	76	2,551	33.6
Drug and Prop.	9	687	76.3	13,740	27	1,327	49.1
Other Retail	23	1,975	85.9	39,500	102	6,506	63.8
Non-Store Retail	14	829	59.2	16,580	31	2,072	66.8
				1,018,280			

*Sales in thousands of dollars   (Source: State Economic Abstract)

Table 3.6. Wholesale Trade and Service Taxes Collected for County A and the Five-County Area During the Past Fiscal Year

Wholesale Trade

	Number	Payroll*	Payroll Tax*	Employees	Sales*	Sales Tax*	Average Sales*
County A	33	387	3.87	142	10,204	204.08	309.2
Area	127	1,566	15.66	460	31,780	635.60	250.2

Service Establishments

	Number	Payroll*	Payroll Tax*	Receipts*	Tax on Receipts*	Average Receipts*
County A	98	425	4.25	2,678	53.56	27.3
Area	400	2,566	25.66	8,143	162.86	20.4

*In thousands of dollars

Table 3.7. Occupational Characteristics by Sex of Labor Force

	County A %		Area %		State %	
Occupation	Male	Female	Male	Female	Male	Female
Prof., Tech.	6.6	6.5	5.5	10.9	7.6	12.0
Managerial	8.9	8.9	8.6	3.3	9.6	3.7
Clerical, Sales	7.4	7.4	8.8	20.0	5.3	28.9
Skilled	31.1	31.3	17.7	12.0	26.9	14.0
Unskilled	14.5	14.5	27.4	44.7	32.7	35.7
Not Reported and Farms	31.5	31.4	32.0	9.1	17.9	5.7

than an unskilled labor force. Table 3.7 provides a
comparison of the characteristics of the labor force
by occupation and sex in County A, the area, and the
state. The skilled labor force of County A exceeds
the area and the state; hence, we can expect the county
to be more supportive of public services than the area
and the state. This comparison reveals the occupation
profile and provides an estimate of potential labor
force of trained workers.

In addition to the descriptive statistics outlined
in the preceding sections, the planning document should
provide an inventory of hospitals, public facilities,
motels and hotels, churches, basic social services,
and recreational facilities. A description of available institutions of higher education, community colleges, and vocational or technical schools should also
be included. In addition, the types of roads and highways, air and water transportation capabilities, and
ground transportation to and from the area should be
analyzed. If we find generally positive indicators
among the various segments of the community outlined
and discussed up to this point, we can hypothesize
that the ability of the area of study to support public
services is good. Since we are concerned with the
ability and willingness of the county to support public
education and public service policies, the next section
is devoted to the methods of assessing financial
resources.

THE FINANCIAL ABILITY OF A COMMUNITY

In any study of ability to support public services
and education policies, the planner will find variation
among communities within the study area. Furthermore,
the impact of state and federal money may vary according to state funding formulae and federal laws. Thus,
one of the first data sets to be investigated is the
sources of revenue as illustrated in Table 3.8. Note
the decline in federal funds and compare this with the

Table 3.8.   Sources of Revenue for County A Schools

Year	County A %	State %	Federal %
-4	20.9	67.5	11.6
-3	23.1	69.3	7.6
-2	26.9	65.9	7.2
-1	27.3	69.8	2.9
Present	29.9	67.6	2.5

increase of county funds over the five-year period.
If no modification has occurred in the state funding
formulae over the span of years illustrated in Table
3.8, we can conclude that the fluctuation of state
money is perhaps related to the variation in county
average daily school attendance. When presenting a
table of this nature in an actual study, it is recommended that the amount of funds be included. With
respect to Table 3.8, however, we shall assume that
the county has been providing additional revenue each
year over the five-year span.

What are the sources of revenue within the county?
The answer to this question will reveal, among other
things, the ability to support and the attitude and
philosophy toward public education. In Table 3.9 we
reveal the major categories for local support of public education in County A. The property tax provides
88 percent of the total support for education; hence
we may wish to compare this statistic over several
years with the maximum possible tax levy for education.
We are simply reporting what is prevalent within the
United States. Perhaps the best approach to analysis
is a comparison of present and past support with what
is possible under the current tax laws of the state
and county. For example, if we find that County A is
supporting education at the maximum rate, our attention may be turned to the alternatives of raising the

Table 3.9.   Local Sources of Revenue Receipts for Schools
              Within County A (Excluding Sales Tax and
              Payroll Tax)

Source	Amount	Percentage
Property taxes from school levies-present	$1,766,860	88
Taxes from school levies-delinquent:		
County Trustee	7,971	*
County Clerk	14,754	01
Interest and penalties on delinquent county school taxes	3,936	*
Payments in lieu of taxes (state and federal)	142,793	07
County privilege taxes, licenses, fines and fees	34,813	02
County liquor tax	23,486	01
Total	$1,994,613	
Total from other local sources	12,184	*
Total from all sources	$2,006,797	

* less than .01

assessed valuation of property, increasing the tax rate, or seeking other revenue sources for needed funds.

What percent of all local tax revenue is applied to financing the public schools of County A? Attacking the problem in this manner is perhaps a better approach toward revealing ability and attitude than merely illustrating how the amount of money was obtained. The planner should consult county tax records, state tax records, county courthouse records, the state department of education, and the local education agency when obtaining data for purposes of comparison. Obviously, many records will need to be explained to the planner, since each county tends to vary in the style of reporting. Although records of this nature are public information, there is often great resistance from record keepers in revealing the truth about the actual sources of the tax money. Frequently, the state teachers association compiles good comparative data on tax rate per pupil, but these agencies are sometimes biased toward certain programs, and the planner may wish to verify these data prior to forecasting needed changes in areas of support. Often state and local agencies juggle formats of their reports from year to year by design, through ignorance, or both. Frequently the total that the planner thought to be the "real thing" turns out to be false for various reasons or nonsense such as, "We got a new computer," "I just took this job and don't know what's going on either," "Our latest data set just went to the printer," or "Come back in six months and we will have your data ready." One tip to the beginning planner-analyst: The secretary of the boss generally knows more about what went where than does the boss. Gaining the confidence of the clerks and secretaries of an agency is perhaps the best approach to obtaining reliable data.

Since we are concerned with ability and willingness to pay for public education, our analysis should continue toward the comparison between total taxes for education and the total taxes for all public services. An analysis of assessed valuation of property and tax rates for education is useful. But, if assessment increases and rate decreases, or vice versa, which is frequently the case, we have no true comparative data set. Local and state politics frequently cause strange changes in valuation and tax rates; hence our best approach to a sound analysis would be to compare the total of all local revenue for public services with total local revenue for schools. This total includes sales taxes, those shown in Table 3.8, and all other sources of revenue.

A comparison between total revenue for public ser-

vices and total revenue for public schools is revealed
for hypothetical County A in Table 3.10. The trend
shown in the column headed "percentage of total received by schools" is positive for education. But is
this trend a true picture of support? What if the
total student population has increased to the point
that less revenue per pupil is being spent presently
than five years ago? How much of this total is applied to capital outlay and debt service?

A comparison of local revenue per student in
County A is shown in Table 3.11. Capital outlay includes items such as expenditure for land and construction or improvement in buildings and the cost
of leasing property, while debt service includes items
such as the interest on loans and the requirements for
retiring debts. If we assume that all the revenue is
spent per year, then the local revenue per student in
all probability is the local expenditure per student.
We shall make this assumption in the remainder of our
analysis. The column entitled "local revenue for
school expense per student" in Table 3.11 includes the
money needed for instruction, administration, plant
operation and maintenance, fixed charges, and auxiliary service (transportation). County A may be in
relatively poor condition when compared to the area
or state since the present $268 must be used in all
the above budget categories. Table 3.11 reveals how
the inexperienced individual may misinterpret revenue
per student. For example, $373 per student may be
quoted to the public instead of the $268 as local
revenue available for expenditure per student. Problems 3.4-3.6 will help us decide on a policy for local
revenue over the next five years.

Problem 3.4. If we assume a 10 percent rate of
inflation per year and further assume that $268 per
student is adequate at present to support the educational program in County A, how much local revenue for
schools will be needed over the next five years?
(Note we are excluding capital outlay and debt
services.)

Solution. The local revenue needed for school
may be determined as follows:

Step 1: First we shall calculate the local revenue
needed per student.

Present revenue = $268

Revenue PY1 = 1.10 ($268)
            = $295
Revenue PY2 = 1.10 ($295)
            = $324
Revenue PY3 = 1.10 ($324)
            = $356

Table 3.10. A Comparison Between Total Local Revenue for Schools and for Public Services in County A

	Total Local Revenue for Public Services	Total Local Revenue for Schools	Percentage of Total Received by Schools
Five years ago	$3,446,429	$1,930,000	56
Four years ago	3,386,441	1,998,000	59
Three years ago	3,333,333	2,000,000	60
Two years ago	3,387,097	2,100,000	62
One year ago	3,269,231	2,125,000	65
Present	3,188,406	2,200,000	69

Table 3.11. Revenue per Student in County A

	Total Local Revenue for Schools	No. of Students	Revenue per Student	Revenue Applied to Capital Outlay and Debt Service	Local Revenue for All Other School Expenses	Local Revenue for School Expense per Student
Five years ago	$1,930,000	5,590	$345	$500,000	$1,430,000	$256
Four years ago	1,998,000	5,680	352	520,000	1,478,000	260
Three years ago	2,000,000	5,790	345	551,000	1,449,000	250
Two years ago	2,100,000	5,810	361	569,000	1,531,000	264
One year ago	2,125,000	5,870	362	590,000	1,535,000	261
Present	2,200,000	5,902	373	620,000	1,580,000	268

$$\text{Revenue PY4} = 1.10 \ (\$356)$$
$$= \$392$$
$$\text{Revenue PY5} = 1.10 \ (\$392)$$
$$= \$431$$

Step 2: Assume the following student enrollment forecast.

PY1	5,900
PY2	5,879
PY3	5,876
PY4	5,890
PY5	5,926

Therefore, the revenue needed per year as calculated in Step 1 is multiplied by the above student enrollment to determine the local revenue needed per year for PY1 through PY5.

Year	Enrollment	Revenue		Revenue Per Year
PY1	(5,900)	$295	=	$1,740,500
PY2	(5,879)	$324	=	$1,904,796
PY3	(5,876)	$356	=	$2,091,856
PY4	(5,890)	$392	=	$2,308,880
PY5	(5,920)	$431	=	$2,551,520

Problem 3.5. If the minimum local revenue required for capital outlay and debt service over the next five years does not exceed the present ($620,000), what is the minimum total revenue needed for the schools of County A for each of the five planning years?

Solution. The total revenue may be calculated as shown.

Year	Revenue per Year		Revenue for Capital Outlay and Debt Services		Total Revenue Needed
PY1	$1,740,500	+	$620,000	=	$2,360,500
PY2	$1,904,796	+	$620,000	=	$2,524,796
PY3	$2,091,856	+	$620,000	=	$2,711,856
PY4	$2,308,880	+	$620,000	=	$2,928,880
PY5	$2,551,520	+	$620,000	=	$3,171,520

Problem 3.6. Eighty percent of the total local revenue needed for schools is generated by property taxes. The present property tax rate for schools in County A is $3.65 per $1,000 (.00365) assessed valuation. The assessed property valuation in County A is presently $428,191,780. Assume that the present assessed property valuation will not change over the next five years. What rate will be required to ensure 80 percent of the total revenue needed to operate the schools over the next five years?

Solution. This problem may be approached in two steps as outlined below. The main purpose for presenting the problem and solution in this manner is to encourage the planner to look at the total environment. Too frequently we find that politicians lower assessment and raise valuation to gain votes, while revenue remains constant.

Step 1: If 80 percent of the current revenue of $2,200,000 needed to operate the schools is $1,760,000, our goal would be as follows:

Year	Required Revenue from Property Tax
PY1	$1,888,400
PY2	$2,019,840
PY3	$2,169,490
PY4	$2,343,110
PY5	$2,537,220

Step 2: Our second step requires the formula $X_1 (\$428,191,780) = PY1$, where $X_1 =$ the tax rate for planning year one, and $PY1 = \$1,888,400$. Thus,

$$X_1 = \frac{\$1,888,400}{\$482,191,780} = .003916,$$

or $3.92 per $1,000 assessed valuation. That is, the tax rate would move from the current $3.65 to $3.92 for planning year one (PY1). The rates for PY2 through PY5 are

PY2	$4.19
PY3	$4.50
PY4	$4.86
PY5	$5.26

The above examples reveal the need for the type of assessment of financial ability presented earlier in this chapter. We have not taken a serious look at expected revenue from sales taxes or local payroll taxes to support education, but a forecast of the total sales taxes, payroll taxes, corporate income taxes, motor vehicle taxes, and other forms of revenue is one activity that the planner must complete in order to develop policy goals for the public service area. Since payroll or income taxes and sales taxes comprise from 6 to 12 percent of total local revenue, the planning document should provide a complete analysis of these revenues. Revenue from the various tax categories, except property tax, is a direct function of the number of jobs available and the employment rate.

The cycle of the economy starts with jobs and payroll. The amount of sales tax collected obviously

depends upon the amount of buying. The amount of buying depends upon the payroll, the level of skill of
the work force, and the education of the work force;
hence, the cause and effect relationships seem to be
endless. The economic cycle complements revenue col-
lections. The revenue needed to operate schools may
be determined as shown in Problem 3.7.

Problem 3.7. Assume that County A has a need to
construct a new facility at a cost of $350,000 and the
current debt claims $620,000 for principal and inter-
est per year. Of this $620,000, $520,000 is principal.
Since the debt limit is $2,500,000 for the public
schools of County A, what would be the total revenue
needed to operate the schools for PY1 through PY5?

Solution. The revenue needed may be calculated
by the following steps.

Step 1: What is the bonded indebtedness of County
         A? If we add $350,000 to the current
         $520,000 principal, we note that County A
         is using only 35 percent of the limit;
         hence it is sound to assume the additional
         debt. Table 3.12 reveals the new debt with
         an interest rate of .0755 and the payback
         schedule for bonded indebtedness over the
         next nine years. For the next five years
         the payback schedule may be summarized as
         follows:

         PY1 $26,425
         PY2 $26,425
         PY3 $26,425
         PY4 $26,425
         PY5 $96,425

         The total amount of revenue needed to cover
         the capital outlay cost would be the amount
         in the above schedule, plus the $620,000
         that is currently obligated. The total
         per planning year would be

         PY1 $646,425
         PY2 $646,425
         PY3 $646,425
         PY4 $646,425
         PY5 $716,425

Step 2: To determine the total revenue needed, we
         add the total revenue needed for operating
         expenses (as determined in Problem 3.5) and
         the payback schedule. Hence, the solution is

PY1 $2,360,500   + $26,425   = $2,386,925.00
PY2 $2,524,796   + $26,425   = $2,551,221.00
PY3 $2,711,856   + $26,425   = $2,738,281.00
PY4 $2,928,880   + $26,425   = $2,955,305.00
PY5 $3,171,520   + $96,425   = $3,267,945.00

Table 3.12.   Principal and Interest
                Payback Schedule

Year	Principal	Interest
PY1	0	$ 26,425
PY2	0	26,425
PY3	0	26,425
PY4	0	26,425
PY5	70,000	26,425
PY6	70,000	21,140
PY7	70,000	15,855
PY8	70,000	10,570
PY9	70,000	5,285
	350,000	$184,975

Problem 3.7 presents some new concerns for the policy planner regarding bonded indebtedness. There are problems of ability to pay, problems of selling bonds at the appropriate time, problems of bond rating, problems of the sales procedures, and budgeting over the 10, 20, or 30 years allowed to amortize the issues. These and many other significant problems related to bonding are discussed by Stollar[11] in Managing School Indebtedness. When any public agency is involved in long term payments, it is necessary for the planner to provide revenue forecasts before the issuance of bonds. Additional problems are provided at the end of this chapter to assist the planner in this important area.

DETERMINING THE PAYBACK SCHEDULE WITH THE MICROCOMPUTER

Part of Problem 3.7 required the calculation of a payback schedule. The computer program entitled "Payback Schedule" presented in Appendix A provides a general approach to calculating interest over several years. As noted in the interactions shown in the following computer example, the four items to be entered are the amount, the rate of interest, the number of years to repay the debt, and the year in which the first payment on principal is to be made.

```
]

]RUN PAYBACK SCHEDULE
ENTER AMOUNT FINANCED.
?350000

ENTER INTEREST RATE.
?.0755
```

```
ENTER NUMBER OF YEARS OF PAYBACK.
?9

ENTER YEAR IN WHICH 1ST PAYMENT ON      PRINCIPAL IS TO BE MADE.
?5


YEAR PRINCIPAL  INTEREST  TOTAL

PY1  0          26425     26425
PY2  0          26425     26425
PY3  0          26425     26425
PY4  0          26425     26425
PY5  70000      26425     96425
PY6  70000      21140     91140
PY7  70000      15855     85855
PY8  70000      10570     80570
PY9  70000      5285      75285
     -------    -------   --------
     350000     184975    534975



RETURN TO DISPLAY 'BALANCE OF PRINCIPAL' DATA.
?0


YEAR BALANCE OF PRINCIPAL

PY1  350000
PY2  350000
PY3  350000
PY4  350000
PY5  280000
PY6  210000
PY7  140000
PY8  70000
PY9  0
```

SUMMARY

This chapter has presented an outline of some of the major variables to be studied in a community analysis. The main purpose of the community analysis was to determine the level of support for education and other public services. An assessment of attitudes and a historical sketch were suggested as a means to determine the level of support and policy trends. Furthermore, the planner was guided through some significant phases of a microanalysis of population and other economic indicators. Problems relevant to forecasting population, the number of jobs, and housing needs were presented. These provided the major base for the final analysis and were concerned with the ability of the community to pay for public services. The final section dealt with forecasting the amount of revenue needed to support education, investigated revenue sources such as property taxes, and illustrated the tax rates needed to support the retirement of public bonds.

The student should note that all the projective data presented here provided the foundation for policy decisions concerning the need for revenue to support public services. One of the major components of the analysis depended on the forecast of student population, the topic of the next chapter.

Although this chapter focused on educational issues, other public service agencies may also use the formats presented here to conduct an economic analysis. It is evident that public service policy making requires many of the variables used in educational policy development. The microcomputer programs used here are found in Appendix A.

Chapter 4
Population
Forecasting
Models

In this chapter emphasis is placed on procedures for forecasting student population. There are many reasons why administrative planners need to forecast student population trends. For example, forecasts are necessary for policy decisions concerning budget requirements, total revenue requirements, personnel needs, program changes, facility needs, and transportation demands. The methods utilized in this chapter are dependent upon data such as present and past enrollments, resident live births, selected historical trends, and expected socioeconomic indicators. Microcomputer models are presented as planning tools to supplement the concepts of forecasting.

Although simple to use, the models presented here yield good short-range forecasts and require a minimal amount of data when compared to many of the more sophisticated procedures such as the economic-demographic regression model.[1] For example, the grade progression ratio (GPR) technique designed for public schools yields an average of 99 percent accuracy for the first year of the enrollment forecast under stable or gradually changing socioeconomic conditions. The procedure yields an average of 95 percent accuracy for a five-year forecast. Obviously, the long-range forecasts (i.e., 10, 15, or 20 years) are expected to have a higher degree of error, even when made with the highly sophisticated models.

Forecasting student enrollment, both short and long range, for a given region is risky, perhaps less risky than forecasting the weather, however. In a sense the planner actually becomes part of the model, because one aspect of the job is to know something about the expected national, state, and regional trends, as well as the historical background of the area for which the forecast is given. Information

such as that generated from procedures presented in
Chapter 3 will assist the planner in making good forecasts. For example, the GPR model requires resident
live births and enrollment data as its primary hard
data input. But, since the planner is actually part
of the model, and expected economic and social indicators are also given consideration, subjective adjustments to the hard data forecasts can become good
educated guesses. Strictly speaking the two hard data
bases required by the model already have historical
economic indicators incorporated within them.

The social aspect of the subjective data base includes the general philosophy of the population. For
example, what kind of educational program does this
district want? This variable is therefore reflected
in the property tax rate, which is still the major
source of local support for public education in the
United States. Hence the hard data base (increasing
or decreasing enrollments and property tax rates) may
reflect the social and philosophical variables. For
instance, it is hypothesized that an extremely high
property tax rate can actually cause a decline in
student population growth.[2]

In the following section we present some variables
that influence student population trends. These factors must be incorporated into either the hard data
or subjective data bases when a student population
forecast is made.

FACTORS THAT INCREASE ERROR IN FORECASTS

Mobility of families and the decline in birth rates
have posed unwieldy problems in forecasting student
population during the last decade. In 1970 there were
an estimated 3.14 individuals per household as compared
to 2.75 in 1981. Furthermore, the shift of population
from the Northcentral and Northeast regions to the
Sunbelt, especially Florida and California, has begun
to influence the enrollments of public schools and
colleges. In the future, nonmetropolitan areas near
cities of over 50,000 may continue to increase in
population, while large metropolitan areas are expected to show decline.[3] At least until 1995 the increase in population near nonmetropolitan areas may
be restricted to the Western and Southeast-Southcentral
regions. During this time, the decrease in high school
graduates may be as high as 40 percent in the Northeast and Northcentral regions.[4]

In areas where population is expected to increase,
variables such as available housing (see chapter 3),
money to purchase housing, and nonpublic schools are
to be considered when forecasting student population.

During periods of high interest rates, housing starts
decline, and if this pattern continues over a long
period of time, people depend upon rental property and
housing developments. During a housing cycle, the
school age population undergoes a change. In the
first phase, between 75 and 85 percent of new dwellings
are initially occupied by couples in the first five
years of their marriage. This usually results in
larger enrollments in elementary schools. Through the
second phase, which lasts about 15 years, the birth
rates are lower. In the third phase, the older inhabi-
tants are replaced by families of lower socioeconomic
status who may have more children. The housing cycle
goes through a stage of blight in phase four and the
blighted areas usually become slums. A larger student
population is expected in slum areas. The fifth phase
of the housing cycle is characterized by urban
renewal.[5]

Economic factors such as rising income and employment influence student enrollment. For example,
Hagemann and Espenshade[6] found that interstate migration is related to increased employment opportunities
for 18 to 64 year olds, while falling income and rising
unemployment induce out-migration. Other variables
such as accessibility through public roads, property
tax rates, zoning regulations, and public transportation also affect student population. A good public
school program and new public school facilities tend
to cause an increase in student population. This
trend has been especially noted in suburban areas as
long as property taxation was not totally out of line
with the neighboring regions.

Many of these economic variables can be lumped
into one compact factor: employment opportunities for
the work force ages 16 years through 65. This is
largely a subjective variable in the forecast generated
from the GPR model. We should not forget, however,
that an element of this variable is also reflected in
the hard data base through enrollment (present and
past enrollment). In some instances more jobs mean
more people and increased student enrollment. But
more jobs do not always guarantee increasing enrollments when there are high property tax rates, high
education levels, and good school programs. For
example, in the late 1970s Oak Ridge, Tennessee, had
one of the highest education levels in the United
States. Furthermore, the city also had one of the
highest property tax rates in the region as well as
an outstanding educational program. But, for several
years the enrollment of the system declined while
neighboring suburban Knox County, Tennessee, experienced phenomenal growth in student population. The
property tax rate in Knox County was approximately
50 percent less than that of Oak Ridge, which at
that time was a difference of about $1,200 per year on

a $100,000 home.   Obviously the statement "know your community," and especially its tax rate and the tax rates of neighboring regions, has special meaning when we take on the hazardous task of forecasting student population with any type of model.

THE GRADE PROGRESSION RATIO MODEL

Several examples will be presented in this section, and each one will reveal some of the advantages and disadvantages of the GPR technique. In Problem 4.1 we shall begin with two sets of data--resident live births and enrollment data. The primary assumptions are (1) the enrollment flow from grade level to grade level will be about the same in the future as it has been in the past, (2) the educational policies in the future will not change drastically, (3) the property tax rate will not change significantly, (4) the employment opportunities will be such that no large in or out migration will occur, (5) adequate housing is available, and (6) resident live birth (RLB) and the death rates do not vary significantly for the school age population.

Problem 4.1.   Assume that there is only one school system within a given county. Our job is to determine the five-year (short-range) forecast of student population for grades 1, 2, and 3. Assume that this represents one of three elementary schools within one school system. The forecast may be completed from the following data for the RLB six years before enrollment in grade 1:

Year	RLB
-4	915
-3	913
-2	808
-1	799
Present	858
PY1	829
PY2	792
PY3	677
PY4	668
PY5	652

Enrollment data for grades 1, 2, and 3 may be found in Table 4.1. The beginning planner may wish to know where data are obtained. The resident live births are recorded by the Bureau of Vital Statistics, an agency usually located near the state capital, and the net enrollments are obtained from the local school system or state department of education. Observe that the RLBs for planning year five (652 in this example) are actually last year's vital birth statistics. Frequent-

Table 4.1. Mean Progression Rate (PR) for GPR Model

Grade level	RLB six years prior to enrollment in Grade 1	Enrollment 4 years ago	PR	Enrollment 3 years ago	PR	Enrollment 2 years ago	PR	Enrollment 1 year ago	PR	Present Enrollment	PR	Mean PR
	915	913		808		799		858				
1		287	.3137[a]	306	.3352	245	.3032	229	.2866	257	.2995	.3076
2		280	--	248	.8641[b]	292	.9542	218	.8898	204	.8908	.8997
3		292	--	293	1.0464	252	1.0161[c]	256	.8767	204	.9358	.9688

a 287 ÷ 915 = .3137

b 248 ÷ 287 = .8641

c 252 ÷ 248 = 1.0161

ly this count has not been fully verified by the Bureau
of Vital Statistics; hence, the most recent RLB may be
an estimate. In Problem 4.2 we shall deal with the
matter of forecasting RLBs in more detail. However,
for the present we shall assume that our data base is
adequate.

   Solution.   The above data are incorporated into
Table 4.1 to facilitate calculations and understanding
of the GPR model. Note in Table 4.1 that the resident
live births (RLB) six years prior to enrollment in
grade 1 are placed above each year of entry into the
educational system (grade 1). This is done only to
facilitate calculations. We shall exclude kindergarten
at this point; however, attention will be given to
this grade level later in the problem. Each row in
the table following the RLBs represents a grade level,
while each column represents enrollment per year followed by the progression rate (PR). The progression
rate from RLB to grade 1 four years ago is 287 ÷ 915 =
.3137, while the PR from grade 1 four years ago to
grade 2 three years ago is 248 ÷ 287 = .8641. The objective of Table 4.1 is to illustrate how each mean PR
is determined. For example, .3137 + .3352 + .3032 +
.2866 + .2995 = 1.5382. Thus, 1.5382 ÷ 5 = .3076,
the mean progression rate for grade 1--that is, the
mean rate of progression from the RLB's to the grade 1
enrollments over a five-year period. Note that there
are only four PRs for grade 2 and four for grade 3.
The mean progression rate from grade 1 to grade 2 is
.8997 and the mean progression rate from grade 2 to
grade 3 is .9688.

   Now that the mean PR per grade level has been
determined, our next step involves the calculation
of the five-year forecast as shown in Table 4.2.
First, to clarify the calculation note that the
column "present enrollment" is shown in order to
establish the base year from which the forecast
will begin. Next, note that the RLB row is shown
directly above the five forecasts for grade 1 and
that each forecast is directly beneath the appropriate RLB six years prior to grade 1. For example, for
planning year 1, the forecast for grade 1 is determined
by multiplying the mean PR (.3076) and the appropriate
RLB (829); therefore, .3076 x 829 = 255. The forecast
of 231 for grade 2, planning year 1, is determined as
follows: .8997 x 257 = 231. In similar fashion the
mean PR (.9688) times the forecast for grade 2, planning year 1 (231) is 244 (.9688 x 231 = 224). This
process is continued until the final projection of 181
is reached for grade 3, planning year 5. That is,
.9688 x 187 = 181.

   We may now give consideration to forecasting kindergarten enrollment since the basic forecast has been pre-

sented. Compulsory kindergarten attendance is not mandated by some states. Where this is the case, great
care must be given to this forecast, since it is rather
difficult, if not impossible, to provide even an educated guess for this grade level. The best that the
GPR model can do under these constraints is to provide
the planner with a one year old projection. If kindergarten attendance were mandated for five year old students, we could simply use the RLB five years prior to
kindergarten entry and the procedure would be as shown
in Tables 4.1 and 4.2. At best, what we have in Table
4.2 is the one year old projection of the number that
should be in kindergarten. Hence, for planning year 1
the forecast for kindergarten should be 244. For planning years 2, 3, and 4 the kindergarten forecasts are
208, 206, and 201, respectively. If we assume that the
RLB six years prior to planning year 6 is 648, then
.3076 x 648 = 199, the forecast for kindergarten in
planning year 5.

Earlier in this chapter we suggested that the planner is part of the forecasting model--in a subjective
sense, of course. Furthermore, we discussed the effects of property tax rates and employment opportunities on school enrollments. Our problem now is to
determine how variables of this nature influence our
short-range forecasts in Table 4.2. Thus, we depend
upon the results of the survey methodology presented
in chapter 3. Assume that in planning year 2 an industry is scheduled to move into the school attendance
area and provide 600 new jobs. This variable is likely
to change the forecast in Table 4.2. How great the
change will be depends on available housing. Assume
that 300 new homes and apartments will be made available in the school's attendance area by planning year
3. Our adjusted forecast would be as follows: 300
households x 2.75 individuals per household = 825
individuals.

The most optimistic estimate would be 825 individuals minus 600 individuals equals 225 individuals,
assuming two parent families. Therefore, a more detailed population survey is completed. The best approach would be to divide 225 by 17, since we assume
that students graduate from high school by age 17.
Here we have allocated 13.24 individuals per age
category, ages 1 through 17 (225 ÷ 17 = 13.24). As
far as the grade 1 through grade 3 forecast is concerned approximately 40 students would be added to
the forecast for planning years 3, 4, and 5. In terms
of personnel for these three grade levels, our most
optimistic forecast would be two additional professional staff members.

The term "optimistic" is indeed appropriate to describe the anticipated impact that the industry will
have. For example, our assumption of 2.75 individuals
per household might be too high. Other factors, such

Table 4.2. Five-Year Forecast with the GPR Model

Grade Level	Mean PR	Present Enrollment	Forecast for Planning Year 1	Forecast for Planning Year 2	Forecast for Planning Year 3	Forecast for Planning Year 4	Forecast for Planning Year 5
RLB six years prior to Grade 1			829	792	677	668	652
1	.3076	257	255[a]	244	208	206	201
2	.8997	204	231[b]	229	219	187	185
3	.9688	204	198	224[c]	222	212	181

a .3076 x 829 = 255

b .8997 x 257 = 231

c .9688 x 231 = 224

as nonpublic schools within the county, could be significant in reducing the number of public school
clients. At least the example provides the planner
with some measure of reality in that we did not plan
for 600 jobs times 2.75 individuals per household, or
1650 - 1200 = 450 individuals in the 1 through 17 age
classification. Frequently, planning for too many
new students has been the problem in growth areas.
Although the agency provides an important service for
a region, the local or state chamber of commerce tends
to overestimate impact of industry. More realisti-
cally, however, the policy planner should consult
with telephone and utility companies for expected impact. These agencies are usually more accurate in
their forecasts than the chamber of commerce. Furthermore, the number of new housing starts is a good indicator of economic impact. Again the meaning of "the
planner becomes part of the planning model" implies
that the planner should know the community and know
it well.

An extension of the GPR model is introduced following the next section on the microcomputer application.
One method for estimating resident live births is also
outlined after the microcomputer interactions.

THE MICROCOMPUTER VERSION OF GPR

The preceding problem may be worked with the microcomputer model entitled "Grade Progression Ratio Model"
found in Appendix A. When the program is requested,
the instructions shown in the following example will appear on the screen. After each "?" simply enter the
numbers from the problem. Since there are only three
grade levels, "1" is entered for grades 4 through 12.
This feature may be modified with only a few changes
in the program.

```
ENTER RESIDENT LIVE BIRTH DATA FOR LAST TEN YEARS
    BEGINNING WITH OLDEST DATA
?915
?913
?808
?799
?858
?829
?792
?677
?668
?652
ENTER ENROLLMENT DATA FOR FOUR YEARS AGO BEGINNING WITH GRADE ONE
?287
?280
?292
?1
?1
?1
?1
?1
?1
?1
```

```
?1
?1
ENTER ENROLLMENT DATA FOR THREE YEARS AGO BEGINNING WITH GRADE ONE
?306
?248
?293
?1
?1
?1
?1
?1
?1
?1
?1
?1
ENTER ENROLLMENT DATA FOR TWO YEARS AGO BEGINNING WITH GRADE ONE
?245
?292
?252
?1
?1
?1
?1
?1
?1
?1
?1
?1
ENTER LAST YEAR'S ENROLLMENT DATA BEGINNING WITH GRADE ONE
?229
?218
?256
?1
?1
?1
?1
?1
?1
?1
?1
?1
ENTER THIS YEAR'S ENROLLMENT DATA BEGINNING WITH GRADE ONE
?257
?204
?204
?1
?1
?1
?1
?1
?1
?1
?1
?1
              FORECAST
```

GRADE	PY1	PY2	PY3	PY4	PY5
1	255	244	208	206	201
2	231	229	219	187	185
3	198	224	222	212	182
4	1	1	1	1	1
5	1	1	1	1	1
6	1	1	1	1	1
7	1	1	1	1	1
8	1	1	1	1	1
9	1	1	1	1	1
10	1	1	1	1	1
11	1	1	1	1	1
12	1	1	1	1	1

FORECASTING RESIDENT LIVE BIRTHS

It is often necessary to forecast resident live births when planning for education. Problem 4.2 illustrates one approach to this perplexity.

Problem 4.2.   Estimate the resident live births for planning years 6 through 10 using the following data.

Year	RLB 6 Years Before Enrollment	Year	RLB 6 Years Before Planning Year
-9	296	PY1	308
-8	378	PY2	279
-7	351	PY3	303
-6	328	PY4	294
-5	314	PY5	328
-4	298	PY6	334*
-3	285	PY7	341*
-2	267	PY8	348*
-1	292	PY9	354*
Present	304	PY10	361*

*Estimated

Solution.   Since there is a lag time of at least one year before RLBs are validated by the Bureau of Vital Statistics, it is appropriate to forecast the RLBs needed for planning year 6 as well as planning years 7 through 10. One method of forecasting the RLBs would be to determine the fertility rates for the female population ages 16 through 40 and from this rate forecast the expected RLBs per year. But this method is somewhat cumbersome and depends upon multiplying estimates by estimates. That is, the result would entail multiplying the estimated fertility rate and the estimated number of females in the 16 through 40 year age classification per year over the five-year period. One possible and perhaps "quick and rough" approach would be to use the standard compound interest formula. At least this method would eliminate multiplying an estimate at the beginning (planning year 6). In the problem at hand we shall first determine the rate of change per year over the past five years (over the past 10 or 15 years if a sharp trend is noted) and add this rate, either positive or negative, per year. The calculations are

Year	RLB	Rate of Change
PY1	308	
PY2	279	-.094156
PY3	303	.086022
PY4	294	-.029703
PY5	328	.115646

The algebraic sum over the four intervals is .077809.

This rate divided by four is .019452. Therefore, the result according to the compound interest formula is

$$RLB_6 = 328 (1.019452)^1$$
$$= 334,$$
$$RLB_7 = 328 (1.019452)^2$$
$$= 341,$$
$$RLB_8 = 328 (1.019452)^3$$
$$= 348,$$
$$RLB_9 = 328 (1.019452)^4$$
$$= 354, \text{ and}$$
$$RLB_{10} = 328 (1.019452)^5$$
$$= 361.$$

Here the basic assumption is that the growth rate will be (.0194522374) over planning years 6 through 10. Obviously, it is rather risky business to forecast the mating habits of the female population ages 16 through 40 over a five-year period. Some experts say the birth rate is tied to the economy, which is also difficult to forecast. Our assumption that people are "creatures of habit" is the best one available at this time.

Now that we have determined the RLB data, we can forecast enrollment in Problem 4.3.

Problem 4.3. Provide a ten-year forecast for one school within a county based on the enrollment data and RLBs presented in Table 4.3.

Solution. The progression rates (PR) are determined as illustrated in Problem 4.1. However, in this example each mean PR for grades 2 through 6 is calculated by summing the nine PRs per row and dividing by 9. Ten sets are used to calculate PR over the ten-year period. Once the mean progression rates are specified, the next step is to forecast the enrollment for the ten-year period as displayed in Table 4.4.

Perhaps the most difficult part of the projection model is obtaining the forecast for planning year 1. Therefore the following calculations should be analyzed carefully by the beginning planner.

Mean PR		RLB six years prior to Grade 1			PY1	Forecast grade level
.28384	x	308		=	87	1

Mean PR		Present Enrollment	Present Grade Level		PY1	Forecast grade level
.94028	x	82	(I)	=	77	2
1.01173	x	88	(II)	=	89	3
1.00130	x	77	(III)	=	77	4
0.99431	x	86	(IV)	=	86	5
1.00795	x	61	(V)	=	61	6

Table 4.3.   Enrollment Data and Mean Progression Rates for Problem 4.3

RLB six years prior to enrollment in Grade 1

Grade level	Enrollment nine years ago 296	PR	Enrollment eight years ago 378	PR	Enrollment seven years ago 351	PR	Enrollment six years ago 328	PR	Enrollment five years ago 314	PR
1	84	.28378	85	0.22487	102	0.29060	100	0.30488	81	0.25796
2	90	0.90123	84	1.00000	90	1.05882	94	0.92157	104	1.04000
3	91	0.95192	90	1.00000	77	0.91667	82	0.91111	88	0.93617
4	76	0.98864	91	1.00000	87	0.96667	77	1.00000	92	1.12195
5	90	0.92391	76	1.00000	87	0.95604	89	1.02299	84	1.09091
6	87	0.97619	90	1.00000	70	0.92105	94	1.08046	101	1.13483
Total	518		516		513		536		550	

RLB six years prior to enrollment in Grade 1

Grade level	Enrollment four years ago 298	PR	Enrollment three years ago 285	PR	Enrollment two years ago 267	PR	Enrollment one year ago 292	PR	Present Enrollment 304	PR	Mean PR
1	87	0.29195	95	0.33333	72	0.26966	91	0.31164	82	0.26974	0.28384
2	73	0.90123	66	0.75862	88	0.92632	64	0.88889	88	0.96703	0.94028
3	99	0.95192	88	1.20548	64	0.96970	89	1.01136	77	1.20313	1.01173
4	87	0.98864	95	0.95960	86	0.97727	66	1.03125	86	0.96629	1.00130
5	85	0.92391	89	1.02299	88	0.92632	93	1.08140	61	0.92424	0.99431
6	82	0.97619	89	1.04706	86	0.96629	87	0.98864	89	0.95699	1.00795
Total	513		522		484		490		483		

Table 4.4. Ten-Year Forecast with GPR Model for Problem 4.3

RLB six years prior to Grade 1	308	279	303	294	328	334	341	348	354	361
Grade level	PY1	PY2	PY3	PY4	PY5	PY6	PY7	PY8	PY9	PY10
1	87	79	86	83	93	95	97	99	100	102
2	77	82	74	81	78	87	89	91	93	94
3	89	78	83	75	82	79	88	90	92	94
4	77	89	78	83	75	82	79	88	90	92
5	86	77	89	78	83	75	82	79	88	89
6	61	86	77	89	78	84	76	83	80	89
Total	478	491	488	490	490	501	508	525	536	550

Calculations shown above are based on the mean PR and
present enrollment in Table 4.3 and the RLB (308) six
years prior to grade 1 as shown in Table 4.4. The
Roman numerals listed under the column "present grade
level" are indicators of present enrollment positions
in Table 4.3 and should not be used in the multipli-
cation; that is, 1.01173 x 88 (II) = 89, since the
(II) indicates the grade level location in Table 4.3.
     To forecast grade level 1 for PY2, multiply
.28384 by 279; thus, (.28384) (279) = 79. The forecast for grade level 2 in PY2 is computed:
(.94028) (87) = 82. In similar fashion, the forecast
for grade level 6 and PY7 is computed: (1.00795) (75)
= 76.

     Forecasts shown in Table 4.4 reveal a gradual in-
crease from PY4 through PY10. If we consider this as
a long-range forecast, then perhaps there are favor-
able economic indicators for this attendance area.
That is, we could hypothesize that our long-range
forecast is a function of the expected economic growth
paralleled by steady increases in the availability of
jobs, increased in-migration, and a moderate rate of
inflation. But increasing student population may not
always indicate improved economic conditions. For
example, in some areas of extreme poverty in the United
States the school age population is known to show some
increases during severe depression. This may be a
result of the students' receiving free school lunches.
Furthermore, when jobs are available there is a tendency for decline especially in grade levels 10
through 12.[7] The job of the planner is to study the
forecasts of economists, utility companies, farm
organizations, business, and industry before making
the enrollment forecast. If this method of forecasting is unacceptable and the planner desires more
sophisticated procedures, there are more comprehensive
models available. Unfortunately many of the models
used by economists and other forecasters are not any
better than the GPR model.

                    OTHER FORECASTING MODELS

     In this section we shall use the data base found
in Table 4.3 to forecast student enrollment in
Problems 4.4 through 4.7. This will be accomplished
through the assistance of the standard compound interest formula, a linear regression model (least squares),
and the Bayesian model. The short-range forecasts
from these models will be compared to the actual enrollment in order for the planner to understand the
limitations and advantages of each of the four models

Table 4.5.   Enrollment Data for Problem 4.4

Time	Total Enrollment	Rate of Change
-9 years	518	
-8 years	516	-.00386
-7 years	513	-.00585
-6 years	536	+.04291
-5 years	550	+.02545
-4 years	513	-.07212
-3 years	522	-.01724
-2 years	484	-.07851
-1 year	490	+.01224
Present	483	-.01449

presented in this chapter. The data base shown in Table 4.3 represents actual enrollments collected during a study of a rural school system. Presently five years have elapsed since the forecast was made, allowing five years of actual enrollment for comparison with the first five years of the forecast. Although this is a special case (Table 4.3), where a minimal amount of increased economic activity was experienced and where the resident live births did not change to a great degree, we can obtain basic knowledge of forecasting enrollments from the examples herein and make some valid comparisons for accuracy.

THE STANDARD COMPOUND INTEREST FORMULA

   Problem 4.4. Provide a ten-year forecast of student enrollment using the standard compound interest formula and the data in Table 4.5.
   Solution. First, note in Table 4.5 that the change from year to year is shown under the column headed "rate of change." To determine the rate between nine years and eight years ago, the following calculations are performed: $(516 - 518) \div 518 = -.00386100386$. This task is completed for the ten consecutive years and the algebraic sum over the nine intervals is divided by 9. Turning our attention to the formula (see chapter 3), we note that the base year (enrollment of the present year) is multiplied by $(1 - .00701511877)^t$, where $t = 1, 2, 3, \ldots 10$, to obtain the forecast for each of the ten planning years. Therefore,

$$PY1 \quad = 483 \ (1-.00701511877)^1$$
$$\quad\quad\quad = 483 \ (.9929849)^1$$
$$\quad\quad\quad = 480$$
$$PY2 \quad = 483 \ (.9929849)^2$$
$$\quad\quad\quad = 476$$
$$PY3 \quad = 483 \ (.9929849)^3$$
$$\quad\quad\quad = 473$$
$$PY4 \quad = 483 \ (.9929849)^4$$
$$\quad\quad\quad = 470$$
$$PY5 \quad = 483 \ (.9929849)^5$$
$$\quad\quad\quad = 466$$
$$PY6 \quad = 483 \ (.9929849)^6$$
$$\quad\quad\quad = 463$$
$$PY7 \quad = 483 \ (.9929849)^7$$
$$\quad\quad\quad = 460$$
$$PY8 \quad = 483 \ (.9929849)^8$$
$$\quad\quad\quad = 457$$
$$PY9 \quad = 483 \ (.9929849)^9$$
$$\quad\quad\quad = 453, \text{ and}$$
$$PY10 \quad = 483 \ (.9929849)^{10}$$
$$\quad\quad\quad = 450.$$

The alternate method for calculating each year would
be enrollment one year ago times $(1 + r)$. That is,

$$PY1 = 483 \ (.9929849) = 480,$$
$$PY2 = 480 \ (.9929849) = 476,$$
$$PY3 = 476 \ (.9929849) = 473, \text{ etc.}$$

A LINEAR REGRESSION MODEL

Problem 4.5.   Provide a ten-year forecast of student enrollment using a linear regression model.
   Solution.   The simple linear regression (LR) model,
$PYN = A + BX$, is another possible procedure that would
be appropriate for forecasting enrollment. The basic
assumption for the model is that the forecast will be
on the line of best fit on an x, y axis as determined
from the historical data base shown in Figure 4.1.
Since there are ten equal intervals in the data set and
since 550 - 483 = 67 (the range in enrollment), each
interval is 6.7 enrollment units apart as illustrated on
the y-axis. The ten years of data are shown with respect to "X" in Figure 4.1, where 1 = enrollment data
nine years ago (518), 2 = enrollment eight years ago
(516), and so forth through 10 = present enrollment
(483). That is, when X = 1, Y = 518; when X = 2,
Y = 516; and the sequence is completed with X = 10,
Y = 483.
   First we perform the calculations shown below.
We now determine the coefficient of X in $PYN = A_{yx} + B_{yx}X$. This coefficient, B_{yx}, is also known as
the slope or the regression coefficient. The subscripts
yx denote that we wish to forecast y (enrollment) for
a specific year, x.

$$B_{yx} = \frac{N\Sigma XY - (\Sigma X)(\Sigma Y)}{N\Sigma X^2 - (\Sigma X)^2} \; .$$

Where N = 10, the number of data sets and the other symbols needed for data treatment are as follows:

X	Y	XY	X^2	Y^2	$(Y-\bar{Y})^2$
1	518	518	1	268,324	30.25
2	516	1032	4	266,256	12.25
3	513	1539	9	263,169	.25
4	536	2144	16	287,296	552.25
5	550	2750	25	302,500	1406.25
6	513	3078	36	263,169	.25
7	522	3654	49	272,484	90.25
8	484	3872	64	234,256	812.25
9	490	4410	81	240,100	506.25
10	483	4830	100	233,289	870.25

$\Sigma X=55$ $\Sigma Y=5125$ $\Sigma XY=27,827$ $\Sigma X^2=385$ $\Sigma Y^2=2,630,843$ $\Sigma(Y-\bar{Y})^2=$ 4280.5

Figure 4.1.   Scattergram of Data Base for Problem 4.5

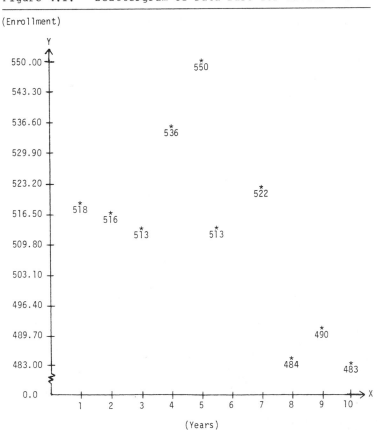

(Enrollment)

(Years)

The regression coefficient is

$$B_{yx} = \frac{10(27,827) - (55)(5125)}{10(385) - (55)^2} ,$$

$$= \frac{278,270 - 281,875}{3850 - 3025} ,$$

$$= \frac{-3605}{825}$$

$$= -4.369696967.$$

A_{yx} is determined as follows:

$$A_{yx} = \text{Mean of } Y - \text{Mean of } X(B_{yx}) ,$$

$$= \bar{Y} - \bar{X} (B_{yx}).$$

By substituting $\bar{Y} = \dfrac{\Sigma Y}{N}$ and $\bar{X} = \dfrac{\Sigma X}{N}$

we obtain $\bar{Y} = \dfrac{5125}{10} = 512.5$ and $\bar{X} = \dfrac{55}{10} = 5.5.$

Therefore, $A_{yx} = 512.5 - 5.5 (B_{yx}).$

Consequently, since $B_{yx} = -4.369696967$ in our example,

$$A_{yx} = 512.5 - 5.5 (-4.369696967) ,$$

$$= 536.533334.$$

The resulting equation for forecasting the enrollment is $PYN = A_{yx} + B_{yx}X$. Since we wish to forecast enrollment for ten consecutive years, x takes the values of 11, 12, 13, ... 20. Hence,

$$PY1 = 536.533334 - 4.369696967 (11)$$
$$= 488,$$
$$PY2 = 536.533334 - 4.369696967 (12)$$
$$= 484,$$

and continuing we find

$$PY3 = 480,$$
$$PY4 = 475,$$
$$PY5 = 471,$$
$$PY6 = 467,$$
$$PY7 = 462,$$

PY8 = 458,
PY9 = 454,
PY10 = 449.

Finally, the standard error of estimate, SE_{yx}, is calculated for the purpose of determining the probability of where each estimate, PYN, will be with respect to each solution for the equation $PYN = A_{yx} + B_{yx}X$. The standard deviation of y is

$$\sigma y = \sqrt{\frac{\Sigma(y-\bar{y})^2}{N}}$$

and R_{yx} = the correlation between X and Y. The formula for the standard error is

$$SE_{yx} = \sigma y \sqrt{1-R^2_{yx}} .$$

The correlation formula is

$$R^2_{yx} = \frac{\left(N\Sigma XY - (\Sigma X)(\Sigma Y)\right)^2}{\left(N\Sigma X^2 - (\Sigma X)^2\right)\left(N\Sigma Y^2 - (\Sigma Y)^2\right)} .$$

By susbtituting from the data base we find

$$R^2_{yx} = \frac{\left(10(27,827) - (55)(5125)\right)^2}{\left(10(385) - (55)^2\right)\left(10(2,630,843) - (5125)^2\right)} ,$$

$$= \frac{12,996,025}{35,314,125} ,$$

$$= .3680.$$

$$\sigma y = \sqrt{\frac{4280.5}{10}} = 20.6894.$$

By substituting in the standard error formula above,

$$SE_{yx} = 20.6894 \sqrt{1 - .3680} ,$$

$$= (20.6894)(.7950),$$

$$= 16.45$$

The SE_{yx} indicates that there is a 68 percent chance of the enrollment actually occurring between ±16.45 of PYN. For example, PY_9 = 454, and there is a 68 percent chance that the actual enrollment ten years from the present will be within ±16.45 of 454. In other words, the probability (437.55 $\leq$ actual enrollment nine years from now $\leq$ 470.45) is .68.

A Linear Regression Solved by Microcomputer. Our microcomputer program offers a quick solution to the above problem by requiring only ten data entries. Type "Run Linear Regression," and after each "?" enter the appropriate data. The result is the forecast PY1 to PY10 plus the standard error (SE), the slope (B), and the "y" intercept "A". The interactions follow:

```
RUN LINEAR REGRESSION MODEL
ENTER NUMBER OF YEARS OF AVAILABLE DATA
?10
ENTER ENROLLMENT DATA FOR LAST 10 YEARS BEGINNING WITH OLDEST DATA
?518
?516
?513
?536
?550
?513
?522
?484
?490
?483
```

PY1	488	SE = 16.4475659
PY2	484	SLOPE = -4.36969697
PY3	480	INTERCEPT = 536.533334
PY4	475	
PY5	471	
PY6	467	
PY7	462	
PY8	458	
PY9	454	
PY10	449	

THE BAYESIAN FORECASTING MODEL

Problem 4.6. Provide a ten-year forecast of student enrollment using the Bayesian model.
Solution. The Bayesian process is a simple and straightforward approach to forecasting. With respect to forecasting enrollment, the Bayesian model assumes that there is a set of enrollment forecasts PY1, PY2, ..., PYN, and each one of these enrollments has some estimated probability of occurring. Out of the set of possible enrollments, only one will occur per year, and each occurrence is independent of all others. Thus, if prior information concerning what might happen is available, then the procedure is amenable to providing a forecast with a given level of certainty. Prior knowledge may be obtained from our expected en-

rollments from the grade progression ratio model, the standard compound interest model, or the linear regression model--all of these models are independent of each other. Since the GPR has been shown to provide accurate projection of .95 or better for a school district with rather constant or slightly changing economic conditions, we shall use the five-year forecast provided by GPR to illustrate the prior distribution of the Bayesian forecasting procedure (BFP).

If we convert the above symbols to the Bayesian terminology PYN = B_i, we may present Bayes' Theorem.[8] Given the mutually exclusive events, B_1, B_2, B_3, ..., B_n, each with nonzero probability, whose union is the sample space, then

$$P(B_i/A) = \frac{P(A/B_i) \, P(B_i)}{\sum\limits_{i}^{n} P(A/B_i) \cdot P(B_i)}, \quad i = 1.$$

The theorem may be illustrated by employing the results of the three forecasts. Thus, from the GPR forecast we establish Step 1:

Year	Enrollment
PY1	478
PY2	491
PY3	488
PY4	490
PY5	490
Total	2437

This set of forecasts is converted into the prior distribution by dividing each independent forecast by the total. Thus,

Year	Prior Distribution
PY1	.196142799
PY2	.201477226
PY3	.200246204
PY4	.201066885
PY5	.201066885
Total	0.999999999

One constraint for the prior distribution is that it must approach one as a limit. The prior distribution indicates that we have some prior knowledge about the future in the form of estimates from a rather reli-

able source (GPR). Furthermore, additional evidence
regarding PY1 through PY5 is available from our other
forecasts, SCI and LR. These models provide additional
knowledge about the five planning years, and we noted
earlier that the LR yielded a 68 percent chance that
each forecast would be between certain limits as de-
lineated by the SE_{yx}. The information provided by
these two models is therefore incorporated into the
sample distribution or the likelihood distribution in
Step II as follows:

Year	SCI	LR	SCI + LR
PY1	480	488	968
PY2	476	484	960
PY3	473	480	953
PY4	470	475	945
PY5	466	471	937

Steps I and II are outlined above and must be completed before Step III, which involves calculating
the joint distribution. The product of the prior and
sample distribution is the joint distribution as shown
below in Step III:

Year	Prior Distribution		SCI + LR		Joint Distribution
PY1	.196142799	x	968	=	189.866229
PY2	.201477226	x	960	=	193.418137
PY3	.200246204	x	953	=	190.834633
PY4	.201066885	x	945	=	190.008207
PY5	.201066885	x	937	=	188.399672

Next, the joint distribution is converted into percentages through dividing each independent product by the
sum of the joint distribution. Step IV provides the posterior distribution that allows us to determine the forecast.

Year	Joint Distribution	Posterior Distribution
PY1	189.866229	.199328999
PY2	193.418137	.203057931
PY3	190.834633	.200345667
PY4	190.008207	.199478053
PY5	188.399672	.197789349
	952.526878	

Finally, in Step V each independent component of
the posterior distribution is multiplied by 2437, the
total five-year forecast from the GPR model.

Year	Posterior Distribution				Baseyian Forecast
PY1	.199328999	x	2437	=	486
PY2	.203057931	x	2437	=	495
PY3	.200345667	x	2437	=	488
PY4	.199478053	x	2437	=	486
PY5	.197789349	x	2437	=	482

The Microcomputer Application to Bayes' Theorem.
There are several places in the above problem where
errors may be committed. The computer version of the
theorem is presented in Appendix A. To utilize the
program, enter "Run Bayesian Forecast." The following
interactions result:

```
]RUN BAYESIAN FORECAST
ENTER NUMBER OF YEARS OF AVAILABLE PREDICTIVE DATA
?5
ENTER DATA FOR PY1 TO PY5 FROM GPR MODEL
?478
?491
?488
?490
?490
ENTER DATA FOR PY1 TO PY5 FROM SCI MODEL
?480
?476
?473
?470
?466
ENTER DATA FOR PY1 TO PY5FROM LR MODEL
?488
?484
?480
?475
?471
BAYESIAN FORECAST

PY1    486
PY2    495
PY3    488
PY4    486
PY5    482
```

The degree of accuracy per model is illustrated
in Table 4.6. The actual enrollment over a five-year
period is shown in column two, and the yearly forecasts
and best level of accuracy are presented in columns
three through six. Note that the GPR model forecast
has the best level of accuracy twice. The SCI model
is closest only once, while the Bayesian procedure is
closest to the actual in two out of the five forecasts.
The linear regression proved to be the best of the
four; however, we should remember that the data set
was drawn from a rather stable population. From the
set of information we may simply conclude that in
this stable situation the linear regression model is
best, although these findings refute our earlier
assumption about the GPR model. More study of these

Table 4.6. Accuracy of the Four Forecasting Models

	Actual			Forecasts	
Year	Enrollment	GPR	BFP	SCI	LR
1	479	478*	486	480*	488
2	486	491	495	476	484*
3	484	488*	488*	473	480*
4	480	490	486	470	475*
5	482	490	482*	466	471
Totals	2411	2437	2437	2365	2398*

*Best level of accuracy

models is needed where various levels of change in growth are experienced.

One possible study would involve the collection of data for ten years. That is, the researcher would actually collect enrollment data for a state or selected counties within a state, for example, by grade by year. The objective of such a study would be to input the first five years of data for the purpose of finding the model that does the best job. What one could expect would be that some combination of models might work best in some counties and show poor accuracy in others. Our contention is that no best model will emerge for every part of the state. Hence, the researcher must look for socioeconomic data to justify one model over another for given conditions and counties within the state. Perhaps we might find some interesting and contradictory results if the worst set of input data were omitted as shown in Problem 4.7.

Problem 4.7. Calculate a five-year Bayesian forecast by using GPR as the prior distribution and LR as the sample distribution:

Prior	Sample (LR)	Joint Distribution	Posterior Distribution
.196142799	488	95.7176857	.199594759
.201477226	484	97.5149774	.203342552
.200246204	480	96.1181781	.200429884
.201066885	475	95.5067706	.199154949
.201066885	471	94.7025031	.197477855

Solution. Here the prior, sample, joint and posterior distributions were determined as illustrated in Problem 4.6. Next the forecast is made by taking the product of each independent component of the posterior distribution, which sums to one, and the total five-year forecast of the GPR model (2437). Thus,

Year	Bayesian Forecast
PY1	486
PY2	496
PY3	488
PY4	485
PY5	481
Total	2437

The forecast from Problem 4.7 is slightly better than the BFP forecast in Problem 4.6. That is, when the Bayesian model contained the worst data set (SCI), our forecast over a five-year span was less accurate. Obviously, we need to conduct some studies to ensure better forecasting models for selected socioeconomic conditions.

What do these findings mean for the planner when

the sets of data are unknown? First one must have
some degree of confidence in a given model. The comparisons made in this chapter were from relatively
stable circumstances regarding economic growth and
resident live births. If we had experienced a sharp
upward trend in economic growth, which model would
have been a candidate from which the prior distribution would have been developed? If the opposite had
been true, what would have been our best selection from
which to develop the prior distribution? We are back
to the question of "what if?" Again, we must stress
that more research is needed.

"What if" will always be present when any forecast
is made. Our best hope for success in forecasting a
ten-year period then depends upon the model with the
best chance for accuracy over the first five-year
period of the desired forecast, assuming we are looking for a prior distribution for the Bayesian procedure. Until proven wrong in studies larger than the
one presented here, we contend that the GPR is the
best model for the job. Following the first ten-year
forecast perhaps the LR model would be adequate to
determine the sample distribution where ten years of
known data are used to determine the equation PYN =
A + BX. The results of the LR model might also be
combined with the SCI forecast to determine the
Bayesian forecast. In summary, here are the steps
recommended to conduct a ten-year forecast with the
BFP:

> Step 1: Forecast five years of resident live
>   births (Problem 4.2) such that a ten-year
>   forecast can be made as illustrated in
>   Problem 4.3.
> Step 2: Calculate a ten-year forecast according
>   to GPR Problem 4.3.
> Step 3: Determine a ten-year forecast with the
>   LR model and/or the SCI model based on in-
>   formation such as that shown in Table 4.3.
> Step 4: Use the information in Step 2 to formu-
>   late the prior distribution.
> Step 5: Incorporate the results of Step 3 into
>   the sample distribution.
> Step 6: Compute the posterior distribution from
>   information determined in Steps 4 and 5.
> Step 7: Multiply the posterior distribution by
>   the total determined in the GPR, Step 2.

FORECASTING TWO-YEAR AND FOUR-YEAR
COLLEGE ENROLLMENTS

Complications begin to arise quickly when the planner moves into the enrollment-forecasting arena of
higher education. Obviously, the resident live births

component of the GPR model cannot be fully substituted
with high school graduates, even in a well defined
service area. There is the problem of transfer students as well as the problem of adults beginning college at one, two, five, or ten years after high school
graduation. Furthermore, the flow of international
students into the United States is expected to account
for as much as 20 percent of college enrollment within
the next ten years. Hence, here is another complica-
tion. The first bit of data that the planner should
collect is the policies of the institution relative to
the above situations. For example, what is the policy
concerning admitting out-of-state freshmen? Is there
a policy on admitting international students? Are
transfer students accepted regardless of their grades
and standardized test scores? What programs attract
older adults?

The above list of questions may be expanded, and
the problem is quite clear, but not so wicked that we
should give up and wait for the freshman class in
September. Perhaps the greatest difference between
forecasting enrollments for public schools and public
colleges is the full time equivalent (FTE) for college
as opposed to the average daily membership (ADM) for
public schools. For example, in college it is possible
for one student to be counted as one or more FTEs. If
an undergraduate student signs up for 18 credit hours
on the quarter system, and 12 credit hours equals one
FTE, we have 1.5 FTE but only one student.

The majority of public college FTEs come from a
specified service area; hence, we shall begin in
Problem 4.8 with forecasting the enrollment for a community college service area. Assume that we are concerned with a community college with a two-county service area where the total public school enrollments,
converted to potential FTEs, are as follows:

Grade Level	Potential FTE
Present Sophomores	2865
Present Juniors	2855
Present Seniors	2840
Seniors 1 year ago	2825
Seniors 2 years ago	2820
Seniors 3 years ago	2800

The FTE information for the hypothetical community
college is

	-2 Years	-1 Year	Present
Freshman	600	620	630
Sophomore	520	520	540

Two questions are apparent: (1) What is the rate of
progression from potential FTE to the freshman year,

and (2) what is the PR from the freshman to the sophomore year?

    Problem 4.8.   Determine a three-year FTE forecast
for the community college freshman and sophomore levels
based on the information outlined above.

    Solution.   The first approach is to formulate the
data as shown in Table 4.7. From the first set of calculations we note that 21.9 percent of the potential
FTEs enroll for the freshman class in our hypothetical
community college. The 2825 potential FTE recorded
one year ago represents 235 graduating seniors one
year ago, the total for the two-county service area.
Obviously, the FTE forecast may be computed by multiplying by 12, the number of required hours to be a
full-time student.

    In Table 4.8 we observe the results of the GPR
model where, for example, the freshman FTE for PY1 is
expected to be 627. The details for calculating enrollment through the GPR model are outlined in
Problem 4.1 and Tables 4.1 and 4.2. The next logical
extension of this procedure is to move to the BFP

Table 4.7.   Data Base for Community College FTE Forecast

	Potential FTE		
	Seniors 3 Years ago	Seniors 2 Years ago	Seniors 1 Year ago
	2800	2820	2825

	FTE Enrollment						
	Two Years ago	PR	One Year ago	PR	Present Year	PR	Mean PR
Freshmen FTE	600	.214	620	.220	630	.223	.219
Sophomore FTE	520		520	.867	540	.871	.869
TOTAL	1120		1140		1170		

Table 4.8.   Forecast of Community College Enrollment

			Potential FTE		
			Present Seniors	Present Juniors	Present Sophomores
			2865	2855	2840
	Mean PR	Present FTE	PY1	PY2	PY3
Freshmen	.219	630	627	625	622
Sophomore	.869	540	548	545	543
TOTAL		1170	1175	1170	1165

where the additional variables may be accounted for in the sample distribution.

Economic variables also play a role in the number of students who attend college. Thus, the same cautions presented for public school enrollment will influence college enrollment--perhaps even more. Transfer students and those readmitted will become an additional problem for the forecaster. Furthermore, special classes for the community come to bear on the total FTE of the college. Since funding formulae for higher education are largely enrollment driven, the FTE forecast is of vital concern for budget, facilities, and personnel planning. The importance of knowing program and entrance policies cannot be overemphasized for the planner. Likewise the planner in higher education must be aware of the impact of economic shifts upon college enrollments.

SUMMARY

Chapter 4 has outlined some of the factors that increase error in forecasting student enrollments at the public school and college levels. Four forecasting models were presented in detail. One microcomputer solution per model was presented. These rather simple and straightforward models were developed and discussed through the problem analysis and solution technique. Eight problems were provided, and each solution was discussed with respect to the social and economic impact upon the enrollment forecasts.

The four models were tested on data from a community where growth was stable. No clear conclusion could be drawn concerning which model is best for any given situation. Microcomputer programs that solve problems in this chapter are presented in Appendix A.

Chapter 5
Planning
and Management Methods
for Program and Facilities

This chapter focuses on the activities needed to formulate educational program policies and the facilities needed to house the program. Program is defined as all the various organizational components required to provide the inputs, process, and delivery of education to the clients of the public school system. Consequently, instruction, administration, and operation and maintenance of the school facility, auxiliary services, and fixed charges are the major support functions of the program specified in terms of budget categories. Obviously we cannot discuss planning for any length of time without bringing up the subject of budget. Furthermore, discussing program and program costs without mentioning facilities costs is absurd. We shall define facilities as the total physical environment encompassing the program of learning activities. Our attention is now turned to the review of some program planning and assessment strategies.

PROGRAM PLANNING

One classic resource devoted to program planning has been provided by Kaufman.[1] He views program planning through five generic categories outlined as determining needs, mission analysis, function analysis, task analysis, and methods-mean analysis. Boone, Guy, and Walsh[2] present a slightly different view of program planning. They not only include the five categories outlined above, but also emphasize identifying, securing, and allocating resources. Brooks, Conrad, and Griffith[3] have taken the approach that program review involves context analysis, identification of goals and aspirations, the analysis of resource inputs, and the organization and utilization of resource

inputs. There are many common elements in the planning
procedures cited above. Establishing goals and needs
is basic to each planning method. Furthermore, decid-
ing "what is" and "what ought to be" with respect to
program is standard in each of the three planning and
assessment procedures.

   We shall assume a situation where our job is to
survey the educational program and assess its philosophy, goals, objectives, policies, and delivery system for the purpose of determining the appropriate
space relationships to house the educational program.
This process is sometimes called a needs assessment
where the need is defined as the difference between
"what is" (actual) and "what ought to be" (ideal).
It may not always be necessary to determine the actual
first as we shall see later. To begin, let us assume
that we have access to the results of the community
and economic analysis--the type discussed in chapter 3
--and that we have suitable information pertaining to
the present and future enrollments as well as the
directions of population growth and the clusters of
density relevant to the area of study (the results
of the models discussed in chapter 4).

   Like the requirements for the community and economic analysis, the study of program and facilities
must have the approval of the governing board.
Approval means the commitment of human resources, fiscal resources, and time. Without such commitment, the
planner cannot get very much accomplished. Ideally
the program and facilities study should involve outside
experts and a balanced cross section of the community
and the members of the educational organization.[4]
The connotation of this needs assessment study is also
futuristic. In the initial phase we determine what
ought to be in terms of philosophy, for example.
Simultaneously, while the search begins for the ideal,
the planner must help the survey committee specify
what exists. Thus, the focus is not only on the present and future philosophies, but also includes a
study of present goals, objectives, policies, and the
delivery system. The delivery system includes the
organization, the policies, the administrative staff,
the instructional personnel, and all support personnel.
Part of the delivery system is, indeed, the facilities where the educational program is offered to the
public. But, there is more.

   We must look carefully at the geographical location
where the program is delivered. In addition, the study
of the history of the community, the population, employment patterns, the economy and other community variables helps reveal the perspective of the community.
Therefore, we make use of the results of the methodology in chapter 3, which may also be called a context
analysis.

A PROGRAM PLANNING MODEL

When we have obtained a perspective of the community, our attention can be directed toward analysis of
the program and facilities. Figure 5.1 presents an
overview of a basic program planning model that emphasizes the requisite to always know how much financial
support is available or how much human and fiscal support can reasonably be expected. This model may be
somewhat different from the many program planning
models that exist, but the beginning planner will
develop a special appreciation for this planning approach when using it to meet the reality of politics
and other competing forces in the "real world."
Idealism is not or should not be discouraged when
planning, but planning is not and never has been
synonomous with idealism; neither is idealism necessarily futuristic.
    The attitude of a given community toward educa-
tion can be assessed to a large degree through the
philosophical components of the model shown in Figure
5.1. Suppose that we study the educational program,
facilities, and resources of a community and find them
to be adequate presently and for PY5 through PY30.
This is Alternative I, that is, no need exists, or we
have found a situation where the actual is also the

Figure 5.1.   A Basic Program Planning Model

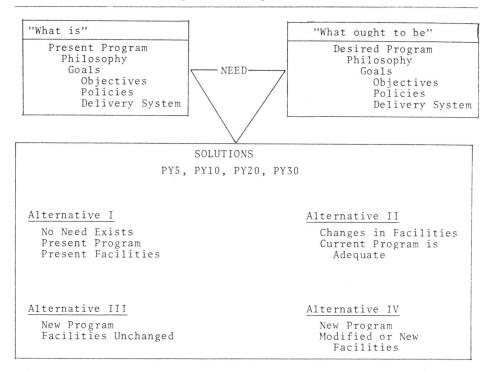

ideal. On the other hand, let us assume that our analysis reveals an adequate program, yet because of increasing enrollments, for example, we must modify the
existing facilities or construct new ones. From this
case Alternative II results, and we must ask the community to provide a different level of support than
for Alternative I. Alternative III emerges when a
new program is installed in the existing facilities.
Obviously, we expect the required resources to be different and to be increased from the present through
PY30 when compared to Alternative I. The fourth alternative assumes a new program and new or modified
facilities. In all probability this alternative will
require more resources (from the present through PY30)
than the other alternatives. Other possible influences
on decisions resulting from the model would, for example, revolve around cost trade-offs between new energy-
efficient facilities and old buildings that waste
energy.

A study of the present program involves the general
categories of philosophy, goals, objectives, policies,
and the delivery system. Regarding philosophy, the
planner should make a comparison of the written
philosophy and the results of the context analysis.
Unfortunately we may find that the present written
philosophy of education in no way represents the attitude of the community toward education. If the written philosophy is to be valid, it should reflect the
attitudes of the community. The theoretical elements
of the philosophy should reveal the way that the educational program should be delivered. Regardless of
what is written, in the long run the only real test
of the philosophy is the size of local human and fiscal resources allocated for the educational program.
Ideally the planner should find a close parallel between program support and philosophy.

Once we accept the present philosophy or develop
a new one, our attention may be turned to the development or modification of primary goals and policies
dealing with instruction, organization, and program
delivery. A goal is a statement of general intent.
Primary goals should complement the philosophy. They
describe the expected long-range results of a program,
are perhaps ideal but attainable, and do not delineate
a specific time for their being realized. The primary
goals of an organization help to categorize the philosophy of a system. For example, we may find that the
primary goals of a local school district deal with instruction, scholarship, and community service. The
support goals are concerned with areas such as faculty,
program offerings, the facilities, governance by students, and the administration. Support goals should
complement the primary goals, while policies guide
the operation and delivery of the program.

A program objective, whether categorized "what is" or "what ought to be," is a statement describing an observable action or a measurable change within a given time frame. The objective basically describes when and where an action takes place and is relatively short range as compared with a goal, which is long range. Figure 5.2 provides an example of the relationships between philosophy and goals and between goals and objectives. This single cross section of a total program reveals the total picture for one objective and how it complements the philosophy. The test of whether the objective is or will actually be put into operation revolves around the cost. If the objectives are acceptable to the community, the philosophy may also be correct. On the other hand, if the objectives are rejected because of the lack of resources, then the statement of philosophy is, indeed, bogus.

Figure 5.2.   An Example of the Relationships Between
              Philosophy and Goals and Between Goals
              and Objectives

Philosophy

   The basic philosophy of this community's schools is to improve the quality of life by developing the capacity for better understanding, thinking, taking action, and encouraging community involvement of teachers and students.

Primary Goals

   Service. To continue as well as enrich the quality of community service.

Support Goals

   Faculty. To carry forward and enlarge support for individual rights and appropriate community service.
   Program offerings. To sustain and enrich the number and quality of academic and support systems including easy access to and assistance in using library materials, computers and other technical support systems, and community recreation areas.
   Students. To maintain and increase individual development, access to counseling, student support services, and support of academic goals.

Operational Objectives

   Faculty member. To engage in at least one community-oriented activity per year sufficient to warrant intensive student involvement (sponsor high school soccer club).

Costs (one faculty member)	Present	PY1,etc.
Telephone calls	$25.00	$25.00
Materials	15.00	20.00
Stamps	50.00	60.00
Five days released time (Substitute teacher)	250.00	300.00
Total	$340.00	$405.00

The program analysis pertaining to philosophy, goals, and objectives is complex and may require a minimum of one year for initial completion. A system of continuous review, perhaps akin to MBO (management by objectives) or a modified form of MBO[5] is recommended if we are to determine whether there is a difference between the actual and the ideal. When goals and objectives are presented in terms of cost, we have a basis for setting tentative priorities. Obviously there is little need to establish priorities unless we know or have a reasonable estimate of the total cost for implementation and operation. The Delphi[6] process is suggested as a means for establishing goals and objectives and setting priorities. With this process, which involves a representative cross section of the community, the students, and professional staff, the planner should expect goals, objectives, and priorities that are realistic and affordable. The Delphi process is a good example of the rational-transactive theory at work. One advantage to representative involvement is that the survey committee, upon setting priorities, has an obligation to support the program changes and work toward obtaining financial support for the new program. Before we can completely finalize these tentative priorities for the program we must know how much space is required to house the new or modified program and whether or not the existing facilities, energy costs notwithstanding, will allow the goals and objectives to be realized.

BASIC PROCEDURES IN FACILITIES ASSESSMENT AND PLANNING

Assume that we have agreement regarding the desired program priorities and that we also have long-range forecasts of the expected enrollment trends, population densities, and economic capabilities of our community. Our attention is now directed to determining the required instructional and service spaces for the proposed program. Although the Council of Educational Facility Planners, International, provides a variety of documents for use in planning and evaluating school facilities, there are two additional major documents that the planner should have. These are the annotated state code and the rules, regulations, and minimum standards for school attendance centers, school sites, and construction of school buildings. These are obtained from the state department of education. Additional information concerning planning and evaluating educational facilities are provided by Castaldi and McGuffey.[7] At this stage we are not necessarily concerned with the existing facilities as much as with

what we actually need in terms of space for housing
the program that has been designed.

Our job now centers around determining the actual
courses and activities that are needed to reach the
goals and objectives defined in the program analysis.
The forecast per course is based on the percentage of
the total school enrollment expected for each course.
This input comes from professional staff and expected
community trends. Let us restrict our planning activities to a high school, grades 10 through 12, where we
expect 550 students in planning year 10 and approximately 950 students in PY20 and PY30. We follow the
outline of the program and liberal space requirements
shown in Table 5.1. This program could perhaps represent the needs for one community requiring only one
high school. We shall assume a seven-period school
day and that each teaching station will be available
six periods per day to minimize conflicts in scheduling.[8] For example, consider the English schedule
outlined in Table 5.1. The state permits up to 30
students per section, and the minimum number of rooms
required for English is determined as follows:

$$\text{Required Room(s)} = \frac{\sum \left[\begin{array}{l} \text{No. of sections requiring 1} \\ \text{period/day, 1 room each} \end{array} \right] (\text{hours/week})}{(6 \text{ periods/day}) \ (5 \text{ hours/week})}$$

Thus, the minimum number of rooms needed for English
is 70 ÷ 30 = 2.33. In Table 5.1 we note that this process is followed for each individual program component.
For example, the basic academic program consists of
English, social studies, foreign languages, mathematics, science, and health components.

One purpose of Table 5.1 is to allow the survey
staff to look into the future. Our calculations are
based on the maximum expected number of students from
the present to PY30. We should make the calculations
as illustrated in Table 5.1 for the present, PY10,
PY20, and PY30. Since bonds for construction are
usually issued for 10, 20, or 30 years, our planning
cycle should parallel this sequence in order to antici-
pate a realistic cost.

CALCULATING FACILITIES REQUIREMENTS WITH THE COMPUTER

In the above formula we have calculated the need
for facilities in an English program. This formula
may be applied to all disciplines as shown in Table
5.1. Note that the end result depends upon program
and enrollment expectations. Quantitative and quali-
tative information are involved in the planning and
decision-making process. By following the example

Table 5.1. Expected Enrollment and Minimum Room Requirements for 950 Students (Grades 10-12)

Course	Enrollment PY20	Number of Sections	Hours per Week	Sections Times Hours per Week	Rooms Required
English (30 per section)					
English 10 I	94	3	5	15	.500
English 10 II	62	2	5	10	.333
English 11 I	96	3	5	15	.500
English 11 II	60	2	5	10	.333
English 12 I	58	2	5	10	.333
English 12 II	56	2	5	10	.333
Total				70	2.33
Social Studies (30 per section)					
W. History I	98	3	5	15	.500
W. History II	64	2	5	10	.333
Am. History I	95	3	5	15	.500
Am. History II	81	3	5	15	.500
Am. History III	48	2	10	20	.666
Total				75	2.50
Foreign Languages (30 per section)					
Latin I	55	2	5	10	.333
Latin II	28	1	5	5	.166
French I	49	2	5	10	.333
French II	22	1	5	5	.166
Spanish I	61	2	5	10	.333
Spanish II	26	2	5	10	.333
Total				50	1.67
Mathematics (30 per section)					
Gen. Math I	75	3	5	15	.500
Gen. Math II	56	2	5	10	.333
Algebra I	61	2	5	10	.333
Algebra II	50	2	5	10	.333
Plane Geo.	30	1	5	5	.166
Algebra III	25	1	10	10	.333
Sol. Geo.	25	1	5	5	.166
Total				65	2.17
Science (30 per section)					
Gen. Sci.	80	3	5	15	.500
Phy. Sci.	52	2	5	10	.333
Bio. I	83	3	5	15	.500
Bio. II	46	2	10	20	.666
Chem. I	48	2	5	10	.333
Chem. II	25	1	10	10	.333
Physics I	20	1	5	5	.166
Physics II	18	1	10	10	.333
Total				95	3.17
Business (30 per section)					
Gen. Bus.	55	2	5	10	.333
Bus. & Econ.	30	1	5	5	.166
Typing I	94	3	5	15	.500
Typing II	50	2	10	20	.666
Bookkeeping I	50	2	5	10	.333
Bookkeeping II	20	1	10	10	.333
Total				70	2.33

(continued)

Table 5.1 (continued)

Course	Enroll-ment PY20	Number of Sections	Hours per Week	Sections Times Hours per Week	Rooms Required
Home Economics (25 per section)					
Home Ec. I	105	4	5	20	.666
Home Ec. II	50	2	10	20	.666
Home and Family	30	1	5	5	.166
Dietetics	27	1	5	5	.166
Total				50	1.67
Art (30 per section)					
Art I	65	2	5	10	.333
Art II	31	1	10	10	.333
Total				20	.67
Music (40 per section)					
Choir	125	3	3	9	.300
Glee Club	30	1	3	3	.100
Mus. Appreciation	118	3	3	9	.300
Band	80	4	4	16	.533
Total				37	1.23
Industrial Arts (25 per section)					
Electronics	45	2	5	10	.333
Graphic Arts	28	1	5	5	.166
Wood Working	25	1	5	5	.166
Mechanical Drawing I	30	1	4	4	.133
Mechanical Drawing II	25	1	8	8	.266
Total				32	1.07
Health (30 per section)					
Health I	95	3	5	15	.500
Health II	63	2	5	10	.333
Total				25	.83
Physical Education (40 per section)					
PE I	245	8	5	40	1.333
PE II	115	3	4	12	.400
Driver Ed.	50	2	4	8	.266
Total				60	2.00
Agriculture (20 per section)					
Ag. I	35	2	5	10	.333
Ag. II	20	1	10	10	.333
Ag. III	15	1	10	10	.333
Horticulture	45	2	5	10	.333
Total				40	1.33
Special Education (15 per section)					
	25	2	5	10	.33
Total				10	.33

in Table 5.1 and using the microcomputer program
shown in Appendix A, the following interactions
result:

```
]RUN FACILITY REQUIREMENTS
Enter the Department name
?ENGLISH

Enter the number per section
?30
Enter the number of courses offered in ENGLISH
?6
Enter course title
?ENG 10I
Enter the expected enrollment
?94

Enter the number of hours class is to meet per week
?5
Enter course title
?ENG 10II
Enter the expected enrollment
?62

Enter the number of hours class is to meet per week
?5
Enter course title
?ENG 11I
Enter the expected enrollment
?96

Enter the number of hours class is to meet per week
?5
Enter course title
?ENG 11II
Enter the expected enrollment
?60

Enter the number of hours class is to meet per week
?5
Enter course title
?ENG 12I
Enter the expected enrollment
?58

Enter the number of hours class is to meet per week
?5
Enter course title
?ENG 12II
Enter the expected enrollment
?56

Enter the number of hours class is to meet per week
?5
```

DEPARTMENT OF ENGLISH

Course	Enroll-ment	# of sects	Hours/week	Rooms req.
ENG 10I	94	3	5	.5
ENG 10II	62	2	5	.333
ENG 11I	96	3	5	.5
ENG 11II	60	2	5	.333
ENG 12I	58	2	5	.333
ENG 12II	56	2	5	.333
				2.33

The computer output in the example parallels the
data shown in Table 5.1. Since these are long-range,
expected enrollments, we note a futuristic element in
the process of determining the number of rooms required. The computer program is designed to accommodate the name of the department, the number of students allowed per section, the course name, and the
number of hours that class is required to meet per
week.

SPACE REQUIREMENTS

Table 5.2 is an extension of the planning activity
presented in Table 5.1. Tables of this nature should
be determined with the assistance of an architect who
has a suitable knowledge base in educational programs.
Our examples are of conceptual cases. It is important
to keep in mind that planning takes place with the
knowledge of community needs, enrollment forecasts and
densities, and the community resources that will be
available through PY30. Table 5.2 reveals the contribution of the architect, for example, in adding storage
space and lab space. We note another contribution of
the architect in art, where two 1,000 square-foot rooms
may be changed to one room of 2,000 square feet, when
movable walls are included in the general design.

A summary of space requirements in terms of square
feet is shown in Table 5.3. The approximate gross is
1.35 times 97,670 square feet or 131,854 square feet.
The gross area allows for such spaces as hallways,
storage, thickness of walls, bathrooms, heating and
cooling equipment, and custodial stations. When the
facilities have the maximum expected enrollment of 950
students, we note that there are approximately 103 net
square feet per student. The range in net square feet
per high school student is generally from 85 to 105.
If we assume a cost of $63.92 per square foot for con-
struction, then our hypothetical school would cost
$8,408,036.80 or $8,850 per student. This cost includes the site and furnishings. Site selection is
discussed in chapter 6. Later in this chapter we
shall provide a long-range plan to determine the local
revenue required to support the proposed program and
this new facility.

The next important step in planning, assuming a
new program and the possibility of new facilities
(Alternative IV, Figure 5.1) is to delineate the space
relationships of the proposed facility. This is accomplished with the assistance of a qualified architect. It is important that the educational planner
work on this phase of the planning procedure to ensure
that each program is appropriately located with respect to the total program. Figure 5.3 outlines an
acceptable diagram of space relationships, and Tables
5.1 through 5.3 specify program and the basis for educa-

Table 5.2.   Space Requirements for 950 High School Students
              (Grades 10-12)

	Classrooms Required	Square Feet per Area	Total Area (sq. ft.)
English, Social Studies, Health	6	800	4,800
Adjacent supply and work area	3	150	450
		Total	5,250
Foreign Language	2	800	1,600
Lab and storage	1	300	300
		Total	1,900
Mathematics	3	800	2,400
Lab and storage	1	300	300
		Total	2,700
Science	4	800	3,200
Bio. Lab	1	400	400
Chem. Lab	1	400	400
Physics Lab	1	400	400
Gen. and Psy. Sci. Lab	1	400	400
Dark room	1	100	100
		Total	4,900
Business	1	800	800
Typing room	1	1,400	1,400
Bookkeeping	1	850	850
		Total	3,050
Home Economics	1	900	900
Sewing Lab	1	1,000	1,000
Food Lab	1	1,000	1,000
Multipurpose (adjacent with movable walls)	2	500	1,000
Storage and bath	1	200	200
		Total	4,100
Art	1	800	800
Arts, crafts, and ceramic studios (adjacent with movable walls)	2	1,000	2,000
		Total	2,800
Music			
Choral	1	1,500	1,500
Band	1	2,500	2,500
Practice rooms	2	60	120
Music Library	1	400	400
Storage	1	150	150
		Total	4,670
Agriculture	1	1,200	1,200
Horticulture Lab.	1	1,200	1,200
Welding	1	800	800
Storage	2	150	300
		Total	3,500
Library	1	7,000	7,000
(one area containing 5 rooms)		Total	7,000

(continued)

Table 5.2 (continued)

	Classrooms Required	Square Feet per Area	Total Area (sq. ft.)
Industrial Arts			
Electronics	1	1,000	1,000
Storage	1	150	150
Graphic Arts	1	1,000	1,000
Storage	1	150	150
Woodshop	1	1,500	1,500
Storage	1	150	150
Mechanical Drawing	1	1,000	1,000
Storage	1	150	150
		Total	5,100
Physical Education, Driver Ed			
Adjacent classrooms with movable walls (4 rooms possible)	2	2,000	4,000
Wrestling	1	1,000	1,000
Gymnasium	1	18,000	18,000
Offices	3	150	450
Girls lockers and facilities	1	4,000	4,000
Boys lockers and facilities (shared with football players)	1	7,000	7,000
Storage	2	400	800
		Total	35,250
Audiovisual			
Work area	1	800	800
Equipment	1	400	400
Films and Tapes	1	300	300
		Total	1,500
Main Offices	2	200	400
Secretary's office and waiting room	1	300	300
Storage	1	200	200
Conference	1	300	300
		Total	1,200
Guidance			
Office	1	150	150
Conference	1	300	300
Storage	1	200	200
		Total	650
Auditorium			
Seating for 600	1	6,000	6,000
Stage	1	1,600	1,600
Storage	2	200	400
Projection balcony	1	200	200
		Total	8,200
Special Education			
Classrooms (movable walls)	1	1,000	1,000
Storage	1	150	150
		Total	1,150

Table 5.2 (continued)

	Classrooms Required	Square Feet per Area	Total Area (sq. ft.)
Food Services			
Kitchen	1	1,200	1,200
Dining	1	2,000	2,000
		Total	3,200
Central Storage			
Equipment	1	500	500
Textbooks and Supplies	1	600	600
		Total	1,100
Health Services			
Nurses office	1	150	150
Examination room	1	100	100
Restroom	2	100	200
Isolation	1	100	100
		Total	450
		Grand Total	97,670

Table 5.3. Summary of Space Requirements for a 950-Student High School (Grades 10-12)

Area	Square Feet
Administration	1,200
Guidance	650
Auditorium	8,200
Library and Audio-Visual	8,500
Vocational-Technical	15,750
Music and Art	7,470
Basic Academic	14,750
Special Education	1,150
Food Services	3,200
Storage	1,100
Health Services	450
Physical Education and Driver Education	35,250
Total Net	97,670
*Approximate Gross	131,854

*The approximate gross area is 1.35 times the total net as shown above. This index ranges from 1.30 to 1.40. The additional area is for hallways, stairways, thickness of walls, bathrooms, etc.

tional specifications. Consider the specifications
for location of the library, for example. The library
is centrally located, yet it is free from noise generated by the shops and music areas. There is a buffer
zone (audio visual) between the library and the food
services area. Also, consider the location of the
special education area. Note that it is located such
that busses with students confined to wheelchairs may
load and unload conveniently. The outside sports
areas are located away from the basic academic area.
Each unit should be planned in order to allow for expansion when needed.

A more detailed set of specifications is needed
before the development of blueprints. For example, we

Figure 5.3.   Diagram of Space Relationships

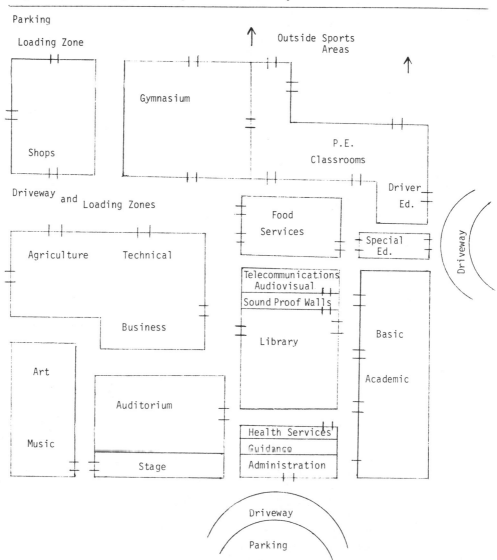

shall focus on the library, as described in Tables 5.1 through 5.3 and Figure 5.3. Before drawing the blueprints, each area should be outlined more specifically according to the example shown in the following section.

AN EXAMPLE OF SPECIFICATIONS FOR A LIBRARY

Philosophy. The high school program should provide a wide range of learning opportunities for the individual needs, interests, and abilities of high school students.

Primary Goal. The library, a vital component of the educational program, has as its primary goal the task of contributing to the maximum educational attainment of the student.

Objectives. The purpose of the library is

1. To provide materials and services for program enrichment, for research, and for reference.
2. To provide resources for the total program and professional staff.
3. To provide instruction and supervision in the use of instructional and audio-visual materials and electronic equipment.

Student Capacity. At least 15 percent of the total student body should be accommodated by the library at one time according to the American Library Association. This, of course, is a minimum standard. Any given reading area should house no more than 80 students. The library proposed in the program described in Table 5.3, for example, is well beyond the minimum standards.

Activities. Some ways in which the library is to be used include the following:

1. Students and the community (after school hours) may use the library to satisfy class assignments and personal interests.
2. Groups may carry on class-related activities involving library materials and equipment.
3. Groups may receive instruction in the use of the library.
4. Audio-visual materials are housed in the library.

Space Requirements. The various uses of the library will require a total of 8,500 square feet distributed in the following components.
Two adjacent conference rooms shall have an area of 1,250 square feet. These rooms will be separated by a movable, sound-proof wall.
The librarian's office and adjacent workroom shall contain an area of 1,050 square feet. One half of the

workroom is designated for students and the professional staff.

The audio-visual area should contain at least 350 square feet and be used for audio-visual storage and repair.

The telecommunications area (850 square feet) should house the school radio station and the central controls for one closed-circuit television station and satellite connection. The necessary auxiliary equipment should also be housed in this area. Approximately 150 square feet of this area shall be used by small groups.

Periodicals storage space requires 650 square feet. Indexed periodicals will be kept for a period of eight years. Others will be retained for two years.

The reading, circulation, and stack area should house one circulation area, three reading rooms, individual carrels, the research and study area, four micro-reading machines, and five microcomputers. Sufficient space will be provided to house at least 25 books for each student. A total of 4,350 square feet is required.

Furniture and Equipment. The following furniture and equipment will be required for the components described above.

Each of the two conference rooms should contain two large conference tables and 20 chairs.

In the office and workroom, space for 1,000 books must be provided with adjustable shelves of at least 12 inches deep and 36 inches between the upright. These shelves will house books for processing and repair. A sink with hot and cold water and a counter with laminated top will also be provided.

The audio-visual storage area will be soundproof and designed for testing and storing of projectors, phonographs, filmstrips, tape recorders, screens, slides, and other audio-visual equipment. One work bench will be needed with dimensions 5 feet x 4 feet x 3 feet.

The telecommunications area will be soundproof and require appropriate electrical outlets.

In the periodicals storage area, provision should be made for storing at least 50 periodicals on microfilm for a five-year period. Shelving should be 7 feet high and adjustable, 12 inches deep, and 36 inches between the uprights. There should be one table (30 inches x 70 inches x 30 inches) and six chairs.

In the reading, circulation, and stack area a circulation desk should be located near the main entrance to service the research and reading area. This area should contain enough chairs and tables to accommodate at least 120 students at one time. Shelving should be according to the standards of the American Library Association (36 inches wide, 7 feet high, and 8 inches deep). Approximately 25 individual study carrels should be provided in this area. Each carrel should contain one electrical outlet. This entire area should be thermostatically controlled to ensure proper materials maintenance and the comfort of the user. Lighting should meet the minimum standards provided by the state education agency.

   Space Relationships. The appropriate space relationships for the elements in a school library are shown in Figure 5.4.

THE ROLE OF THE STATE EDUCATION AGENCY

   Our next major step involves site selection (see chapter 6) and the development of blueprints and detailed specifications. The state education agency is involved in this phase as outlined in the example below:

1. The chief state school officer approves the plans and specifications for the construction of school facilities. That is, in most states it is the duty of the state superintendent of education to determine whether minimum school building standards are being met. The following procedures are typical:
   a. Approval of general preliminary plans and specifications is the responsibility of local agencies. The preliminary plan serves as a general guide by outlining space needs and space relationships. This document should be designed to allow for future expansion if needed. It is accompanied by a map of the area and the site of the proposed location, since it is important for officials and planners to have a complete perspective of the school site and surrounding area. The preliminary plans should also include information such as the type of walks, floors, roof, basic structure, insulation, heating, ventilation, lighting, windows, and doors.

Figure 5.4.   Recommended Space Relationships for the Library

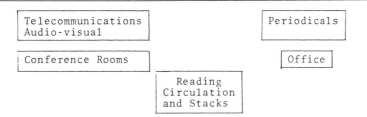

    b.   The final plans and complete specifications including alternatives are approved by the chief state school officer before the advertisement for bids. In most cases the advertisement is preceded by a favorable bond election at the local level. Changes that may affect any component of the total plan must be approved by the state before contractors are requested to make changes.

    c.   In many states the chief state school officer is responsible for submitting at least one set of plans and specifications to the local or regional planning agencies. One of their functions is to check for the environmental impact that the proposed facility will have on the region. When the local or regional planning agency approves the plans and specifications, they may be reviewed by other state agencies concerned with safety and the welfare of the student population. When these various state agencies have made their recommendations and approval, the chief state school officer forwards the final plans to the local school district.

2.   Local school boards are responsible for spending money only on projects that follow state rules and regulations. These local agencies must stay abreast of new state laws as they pertain to expenditure for capital outlay. Expenditure of state capital outlay funds are obligated and expended only according to approved plans. These expenditures are recommended by the local superintendent of schools and approved by the local board of education. Next they are filed with the chief state school officer on or before a given date of the current school year. Before releasing the state capital outlay, the chief state school officer must give a final approval. Tennessee[9] offers one of the best examples of this detailed procedure. Since state procedures vary, the above considerations are given only as an illustration.

EVALUATION OF EXISTING FACILITIES

In the preceding section the focus was on planning a new facility (Alternative IV, Figure 5.1), but we should also consider the possibility of housing the new program in the present facilities (Alternative III). There may be many important alternatives to be considered; for example: (1) What will be the cost of heating and cooling the present facilities? (2) What will be the cost of heating and cooling the proposed facilities? (3) What are the trade-offs in costs between heating and cooling the present facilities and new facilities? (4) Is there adequate space in the

existing facilities to house the new program? (5) Is
renovation feasible in terms of program and cost?
(6) Will the present site be adequate in PY10? PY20?
PY30? (7) Can we meet the goals and objectives of our
new program if it is housed in the present set of
facilities?

Evaluation of the existing facilities should be in
terms of a new or modified set of goals and objectives.
The primary objective of the evaluation is to assess
the adequacy with which a given building facilitates
good teaching and learning with respect to the philosophy of the program. The following basic requirements
underline the evaluation process:

1. The evaluation must assess the relationship between
    the future needs and the present ability of the
    facility or facilities to meet those needs.
2. The evaluation must determine the state of mainte-
    nance and care of the buildings in terms of con-
    tinued operation.
3. The information gained from the evaluation should
    influence the decision to build new facilities,
    operate in the present structure, or remodel the
    current facilities.

Since the evaluation is designed to focus on the
capacity of the facilities to help achieve the goals
and objectives of the new program, the planner should
use the program specifications as a guide. A comparison
should be made between current available space and the
net area needed for the proposed program. In addition
to this assessment, the planner should evaluate the
general structure according to a guide such as the one
shown in Appendix D. This comprehensive outline includes
the major characteristics of most facilities. The
first component is concerned with the total facility,
and the enrollment on a per-grade-level basis. The
more detailed inventory investigates standards with
respect to space. The type of space (defined by the
planner) may be identified as used or unused and the
capacity noted. For example, how many standard spaces
are used in the library? Are there substandard spaces
in use in the library? What is the actual capacity of
the library? When considering capacity, one should
consider the pupil stations, size of the classroom,
plus the teacher station. The rating scale shown in
Appendix D ranges from 1 (missing) to 5 (superior).
If any given component receives a 5, this feature
clearly exceeds established criteria. Both site and
building are covered in the evaluation. There are 12
items for evaluation listed under the site evaluation
form. For each item, the criteria are specified.
The individual building evaluation considers 18 components. If fewer or more components are needed in a
given situation, the planner may adapt the form.

PLANNING A NEW OR MODIFIED FACILITY

The preceding sections have focused on planning according to Alternatives III and IV as described in Figure 5.1. We shall not discuss the other alternatives; however, attention will now be given in Problems 5.1 and 5.2 to extending our long-range plan according to Alternative IV.

Problem 5.1. Assume that the school board of a given school district decides to construct a facility that costs $75 per square foot (this includes site and furnishings) and the gross area to be constructed is 131,854 square feet. If the state pays 20 percent of the cost and the district finances the remainder over ten years with bonds sold at 8 percent, how much will the building cost over the next ten years?

Solution. The total cost to the district may be calculated as follows:

Step I: ($75.00) (131,854) = $9,889,050.

Step II: 80% of $9,889,050 = $7,911,240.

Thus, we find that $7,911,240 must be financed through the sale of bonds. If we assume the rather low rate of 8 percent compounded annually over ten years and payback beginning in the fourth year, we can use the microcomputer program in Appendix A to obtain the interactions shown below:

```
]RUN PAYBACK SCHEDULE
ENTER AMOUNT FINANCED.
?7911240

ENTER INTEREST RATE.
?.08

ENTER NUMBER OF YEARS OF PAYBACK.
?10

ENTER YEAR IN WHICH 1ST PAYMENT ON     PRINCIPAL IS TO BE MADE.
?4


YEAR PRINCIPAL  INTEREST  TOTAL

PY1   0          632899    632899
PY2   0          632899    632899
PY3   0          632899    632899
PY4   1130177    632899    1763076
PY5   1130177    542485    1672662
PY6   1130177    452071    1582248
PY7   1130177    361657    1491834
PY8   1130177    271243    1401420
PY9   1130177    180828    1311005
PY10  1130177    90414     1220591
      -------    -------   --------
      7911239    4430294   12341533
```

Problem 5.2. The current local revenue required per high school student is $270, and our forecast for the high school population (grades 10-12) is as follows:

Year	Number of Students
PY1	559
PY2	588
PY3	627
PY4	642
PY5	671

What will be the required local revenue including the above construction cost over a five-year period if we assume a 6 percent rate of inflation?

Solution. The problem is approached by multiplying 1.06 times $270. This result is also multiplied by 1.06, and so forth. Each corresponding product is then multiplied by the expected student population. Each answer is added to the appropriate interest and principal in Problem 5.1 to yield the revenue required over the next five years:

Year	Revenue Required
PY1	$ 792,884
PY2	811,280
PY3	834,523
PY4	1,981,908
PY5	1,915,107

By adding the required revenue determined above for the cost of constructing the new facility, we find the total required revenue per year over a five-year period. But we have only accounted for inflation, principal, and interest. We have not considered the possibility that the new program might require additional funding. Furthermore, the cost of additional staff and materials must also be included. Obviously long-range planning must entail very minute and rather complicated accounting procedures if our plan is to have any chance of being approved. The board must have a close estimate of the total cost.

Again, we must look to the methods of analysis presented in chapter 3 to find answers to questions such as, How much can the district afford? What are the expected revenues over the next ten years? How much of the total cost will be supported by state and federal funds? The conclusion is that planning requires answers (sound and realistic) that hinge on "what if."

SUMMARY

This chapter has presented an overview of program planning methods tied to methods of facilities planning. That is, we have established the program first, then embarked upon the task of planning suitable facilities.

We have not considered site selection in this chapter
since chapter 6 deals with this important task. Some
major variables that relate to cost were discussed.
The major premise underlying this chapter is that planning without considering the total cost is simply planning for the sake of planning--a waste of time.

Chapter 6
Boundary
and Site Location
Models

State laws specify that the school site shall be
located near the center of geographic areas to be served
and that the sites should be accessed easily. This may
sound trite until one tries to plan for 20 years into
the future. Some laws state that the attendance boundaries are to be drawn such that the concentration of
population shall be sufficient to guarantee a specified
average daily attendance. Constraints of this nature
present location problems for the planner that demand
unbiased solutions. The models presented in this
chapter will facilitate decisions regarding site selection and boundary location. One boundary location
method and two siting models are illustrated in this
chapter. Some of the constraints that may influence
the results of these planning procedures are incorporated into each analysis in order for the planner to
get a better understanding of the impact of rational
systems models on the real world.
  The boundary location models presented here require
two major variables as input: (1) size of population
and (2) the distance between the population centers.
One site selection model depends only upon these two
variables, while the second site location model depends
upon a group of variables identified as location criteria. The latter model is capable of using such inputs as employment, income, accessibility, site characteristics, local revenue, land cost, and environmental factors.
  Various models incorporate these economic and
spatial impacts into planning designs. One such complex and highly sophisticated approach has been discussed by Henry.[1] The first phase of his methodology
employs the use of a regional economic forecasting model

designed by Mulkey and Hite.[2] This phase includes the
employment and income effects, indirect jobs and income
generated from purchases and payrolls, and the spatial
distribution of employment income and population changes
associated with the construction of an industrial
complex.[3]

Historically, the literature has produced some theoretical foundations from which planners may construct
spatial interaction models. Spatial interaction, defined by Cordey-Hays and Wilson,[4] is the interaction
among activities located at different points in space.
These authors regard analysis as the review of goals
and evaluation of alternative plans as a basis for
decision making. The educational planner interested in
site location of public facilities should also consider
the goals of the client before the various alternatives
are presented for approval or modification. When this
is done, the science of unbiased modeling may meet
reality in the form of empirical and experimental research and frequently through subjective decision
making. One example of the importance of integrating
dynamic simulation modeling with research and understanding of population growth has been explored by
Cordey-Hays.[5] This author deals with the consequences
of alternative strategies for growth and change in an
urban environment. Within this chapter an effort is
made to utilize alternative strategies for practical
site selections for public facilities and boundary locations for public school service areas in urban, suburban, or rural settings.

Works by Krueckeberg and Silvers[6] will serve as a
point of departure for some illustrations. For example,
Reilly's Law[7] (known also as the breaking point model)
is applied in Problems 6.1 through 6.4 for the purpose
of generating boundary selections and locating sites
for the construction of public facilities. According
to Krueckeberg and Silvers,[8] persons living in two
towns, A and B, may be attracted to these population
centers directly according to the size of the population (P), and inversely with the square of distance
(d), between the two towns. The boundary between
towns A and B equalizes the effects of population and
distance. Distance according to Reilly's Law may be
calculated with the following formula: $d_A + d_B = d_{AB}$.
For example, the boundary point from town A is
$d_A = d_{AB} - d_B$. The relationship between distance and
population is determined by the formula:

$$\left(\frac{d_B}{d_A}\right)^2 = \frac{P_B}{P_A} \quad ,$$

where P_B and P_A are the populations of towns B and A,

respectively. Proofs of the formula generated from the
above relationship are shown in Appendix C.

DETERMINING ATTENDANCE BOUNDARIES: THE BREAKING POINT MODEL

As a beginning we shall assume a public school district containing two population centers. Towns A and B
are twelve statute miles apart. This hypothetical
configuration will serve as a baseline for discussion
of some of the breaking point model's planning uses.

The first application to be presented (Problem 6.1)
focuses on how to establish attendance boundaries for
the two population centers. Let us assume that the distance between the two towns is measured from the centers
of the two populations. Appropriate data regarding the
population centers may be collected from one or more of
the following: (1) the chamber of commerce, (2) the
regional planning commission, (3) the state planning
agency, (4) local telephone and utility companies,
(5) the U.S. Department of Commerce (the DIME Geocoding
System), or (6) local authorities knowledgeable about
population growth and trends.

Problem 6.1.   Determine the high school attendance
boundaries for Cities A and B given the following information:

	City A	City B
High school student population	1,200	2,000
Capacities of schools	1,200	2,000

Solution.   We shall utilize the formula,

$$d_B = \frac{d_{AB}}{1 + \sqrt{\dfrac{P_A}{P_B}}}.$$

That is, we shall determine the distance from the center
of City B to the point at which the attendance boundary
should be drawn.   Thus,

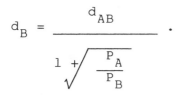

$$d_B = \frac{12 \text{ miles}}{1 + \sqrt{\dfrac{1200}{2000}}},$$

$$= \frac{12 \text{ miles}}{1 + \sqrt{.6000}},$$

$$= \frac{12 \text{ miles}}{1 + .775},$$

$$= 6.76 \text{ miles}.$$

The microcomputer solution of Problem 6.1 follows:

```
  RUN BREAKING POINT MODEL
INPUT NAME OF FIRST CITY:
?A

ENTER NAME OF SECOND CITY:
?B
INPUT STUDENT POPULATION IN A
?1200


INPUT STUDENT POPULATION IN B:
?2000
INPUT DISTANCE BETWEEN A AND B IN MILES;
?12
THE BOUNDARY SHOULD BE DRAWN 6.76209993 MILES FROM THE CENTER OF B
```

Here we note that the proposed boundary should be drawn 6.76 miles from the center of City B and 5.24 miles from City A (see Figure 6.1). Perhaps we should consider some constraints that may enter into the final decision to locate the boundary now that we know "approximately" where it should be. Road conditions, accessibility, and natural barriers (such as rivers and mountains) are some realities that would influence the final decision; we should also remember that politics might play a significant role. Hence, the boundary, in all probability, will not be exactly as shown in Figure 6.1. But it is difficult to find any rational system solutions that do not get modified by special interest groups and organizations. As a planner and decision

Figure 6.1.   Proposed Attendance Boundary
              for the Two Schools

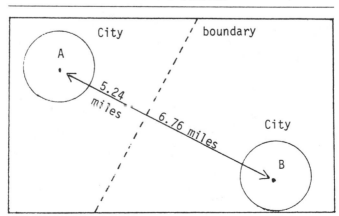

maker in the real world, please expect modifications to
your "systems approach" solutions.

   In Problem 6.1 the centers of population were used
as points for measuring the distance between Cities A
and B. It might be more realistic, depending on their
present locations and the problem, to consider carefully
the locations of the two existing high schools and utilize the distance between them in the formula instead
of distance between the centers of population. Frequently the major reason for determining attendance
boundaries has been for integration purposes. Problem
6.2 deals with both distance and density variables.
   Problem 6.2.   Determine the proposed high school's
attendance boundary based on a distance of 15 miles between the two existing schools and the following information:

	City A	City B
High school student population	1,200	2,000
Number of nonwhites	400	600
Nonwhite density	.33	.30
Capacity of high schools	1,500	2,500

   Solution.   By using the formula in Problem 6.1 and
substituting the nonwhite densities (e.g., 400 ÷ 1200 =
.33) for the populations of Cities A and B, we obtain
the following result:

$$d_B = \frac{15 \text{ miles}}{1 + \sqrt{\dfrac{.33}{.30}}},$$

$$= \frac{15 \text{ miles}}{1 + \sqrt{1.100}},$$

$$= \frac{15 \text{ miles}}{1 + 1.049},$$

$$= 7.32 \text{ miles.}$$

   The solution indicates that the attendance boundary
should be drawn 7.32 miles from the high school located
in City B. This solution assumes that the density (percentage of nonwhites) is distributed about the same in
both the population centers and their suburbs. You may
wonder why such a solution is proposed when there are
many possible perplexities that come to bear. Politics,
pressure groups, and lack of adequate program and facilities in one of the new attendance areas are examples of

these perplexities that may force decision makers to take
another look at the proposed new boundary. The planner
may also wish to seek a more sophisticated model that
would consider the existing capacity of the facilities
or other variables.

On the other hand, it is suggested that the planner
examine the total situation before spending a great deal
of money and time in further analysis. For example,
consider the very likely possibility that regardless of
where the attendance boundary may be proposed and regardless of the model used, the new attendance area may
finally be decided more from subjective decision making
than from the rational model. The planner may therefore
wish to consider the possibility that the pressure
groups, judges, and involved organizations may only be
looking for a place (the planner's proposed boundary)
to start. Providing the necessary object for attack
may be all that could be done, and only the simple
straightforward "breaking point" planning model was
used.

There is no intention to discourage the planner
from being well prepared with fine and very complex
planning models. However, one should be aware that
the groups who investigate the results of rational
planning efforts, in this case the boundary line, may
not understand highly sophisticated planning models,
and as a result they may not place confidence in them
or even in the computer that generated the answer.

SITE LOCATION MODELS:
REILLY'S LAW APPLIED TO SITE LOCATION

An important planning procedure that has direct
application in educational and community settings involves the site location model (see Appendix C). This
model, a derivation from the breaking point model,
assumes distance and population to be in direct proportion, instead of inverse proportion as was the case with
the boundary location model. In Problem 6.3 let us
use Figure 6.1 and the same information presented in
Problem 6.1 to investigate the possibilities for site
location.

Problem 6.3.   Assume that Cities A and B agree
to build a large comprehensive high school to serve
both populations. The site is to be located at the
point most convenient to the populations in terms of
distance from their respective centers. Where should
the new facility be located?

Solution.   First we should take a look at the expected student population 20 years into the future. We
therefore employ the forecasting procedures discussed
in chapter 4 and calculate the following expected student populations:

Year	City A	City B
PY2	1,196	1,978
PY4	1,184	1,926
PY6	1,168	1,905
PY8	1,175	1,927
PY10	1,189	1,952
PY12	1,198	1,980
PY14	1,210	1,995
PY16	1,236	2,015
PY18	1,241	2,070
PY20	1,285	2,120

These population estimates represent the expected number of students in the service areas of each city. Since the expected student population in the attendance area of City B is the larger of the two, it is logical to assume that the new facility should be located somewhat closer to City B than City A. Just how far from City B should the new facility be located? The answer may be determined with the following formula:

$$d_B = \frac{d_{AB}}{1 + \sqrt{\dfrac{P_B}{P_A}}} \, .$$

Substituting the data in our formula we find that

$$d_B = \frac{12 \text{ miles}}{1 + \sqrt{\dfrac{2120}{1285}}} \, ,$$

$$= \frac{12 \text{ miles}}{1 + \sqrt{1.6498}} \, ,$$

$$= \frac{12 \text{ miles}}{1 + 1.284} \, ,$$

$$= 5.25 \text{ miles}.$$

Note the difference between the formula used to solve this problem and Problem 6.1. In Problem 6.3 we have assumed that the population size and distance to the site is directly proportional, but in Problem 6.1 the assumption was that population size and distance were inversely proportional.

The application of Reilly's Law is extended to three sites in Problem 6.4.

Problem 6.4. Where should a community college be located to best serve three communities with the following populations, aged 16 years or older, 20 years from now: A, 20,000; B, 12,000; and C, 7,000? The distances in miles between the communities are as follows:

<u>Distance</u>

	A	B	C
A	--	20	15
B	20	--	22
C	15	22	--

Solution. First we determine the formulae to be used for each of the three comparisons. The formula

$$d_{A_1} = \frac{d_{AB}}{1 + \sqrt{\dfrac{P_A}{P_B}}}$$

provides the relationship to determine the point between A and B, while

$$d_{A_2} = \frac{d_{AC}}{1 + \sqrt{\dfrac{P_A}{P_C}}}$$

assists in locating the appropriate boundary between A and C. The representation,

$$d_B = \frac{d_{BC}}{1 + \sqrt{\dfrac{P_B}{P_C}}} ,$$

yields the best location between B and C.

Substituting in order as presented above,

$$d_{A_1} = \frac{20 \text{ miles}}{1 + \sqrt{\dfrac{20,000}{12,000}}} = 8.73 \text{ miles},$$

$$d_{A_2} = \frac{15 \text{ miles}}{1 + \sqrt{\dfrac{20,000}{7,000}}} = 5.58 \text{ miles, and}$$

$$d_B = \frac{22 \text{ miles}}{1 + \sqrt{\dfrac{12,000}{7,000}}} = 9.53 \text{ miles.}$$

One special case, a graphic solution based on the above data, is shown in Figure 6.2. The site is to be located in some suitable place within the small triangle that is represented by the dotted lines. An alternative graphic solution may be generated by developing subsequent triangles connected at the breaking point and averaging the populations closest to the new point. In either case, we should consider the feasibility of the specific site location, since it is possi-

Figure 6.2.   Graphic Description of Site Location for Problem 6.4

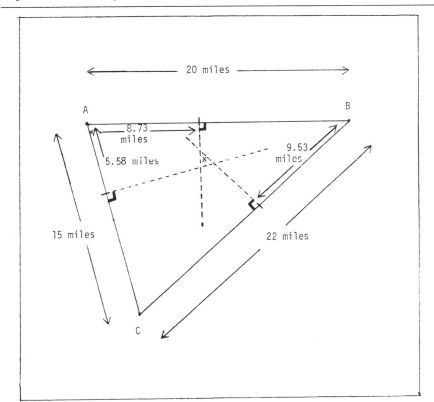

Note: The triangle surrounding the "x" indicates the neighborhood
        designated as most likely for the site.

ble that the final "x" might be in the middle of a
large lake, river, or airport. It might even be on the
top of a rugged mountain. Obviously, these conditions
would require that the planner think of other factors,
such as accessibility, fitness of the soil for construction, and so forth.

When using the graphic approach based on the above
formulae, the planner should take care to ensure pro-
posing some alternative sites near the geometric solution. These would be cognizant of political, geographic, and environmental constraints. If the planner
decides to use the site selection model presented in
Problem 6.4, given several population centers, perhaps
another approach might be to select the three largest
population centers to form the triangle. For example,
if a facility is to be located within a three-county
area, the three centers of density should be considered
as points A, B, and C. The next section presents a
different style of site selection methodology designed
to locate a facility within a given population center
where there are two or more towns competing for the
facility.

THE MODIFIED LAND USE SCREENING
PROCEDURE FOR SITING

The purpose of this section is to provide an alternative to the limited site location model presented in
the preceding section by including such variables as
accessibility, site characteristics, financial ability
of the local community, location of site near population
centers, availability of complementary facilities, land
cost, environmental factors, and so on. This model was
refined and applied by the Oak Ridge National Labora-
tories,[9] and the modification of the procedure as applied to site selection for community colleges was
accomplished by Alvic.[10]

Initially, to apply the modified model, the planner
must determine a list of location criteria acceptable
to the group(s) for whom the facility is to be constructed. For example, when selecting sites for educational facilities, the expected enrollments within the
service area, the accessibility with respect to roads,
the availability of land, the cost and suitability of
available land, the financial ability of supporting
agencies or communities, and the environmental factors,
among others, are to be given serious consideration.
To determine the importance of the various location
criteria, the planner may utilize an opinionnaire or
the Delphi technique to establish scores. Certain constraints contained in state laws pertaining to public
building sites must also be given consideration. For

example, we would not expect to locate a public building near a nuclear plant.

Next, the selected criteria should be weighed,
perhaps through a percentile ranking procedure.
Finally, a suitability score is determined from the
sum of the products of the percentile ranks and the
selection criteria divided by the sum of the percentile ranks. To illustrate the procedures and the
model, we shall solve Problems 6.5 and 6.6.

Problem 6.5. A, B, and C are competing for a
public education facility to be constructed within
one of their present service areas. All three communities will utilize the facility. The towns have
agreed that criteria to be used in determining the
site are <u>distance</u>, <u>availability</u>, <u>population</u>, and
<u>accessibility</u>.

Solution. The first step in solving this problem
is to conduct several research projects. Some type of
opinionnaire and survey concerning accessibility and
availability must be completed. Also, long-range forecasts should be made concerning the age groups that are
expected to use the proposed facility. Ability to support and build the public facility should also be determined, although we will exclude this variable and other
important considerations from our present problem. For
each town the populations that are expected to use the
facility 20 years from now are A, 2,100; B, 1,200; C,
1,320. The distances, in miles, between the towns are
given below:

Distance

	A	B	C
A	–	7	6
B	7	–	5
C	6	5	–

One major step in the solution involves determining
the weights, W_{Ci}, of the four criteria. Hence, through
a survey instrument administered to a representative
group of citizens, we obtain scores per criteria as
follows:

Location Criteria (C_i)	Score	Rank
Distance (C_1)	275	1
Availability (C_2)	175	4
Population (C_3)	215	2
Accessibility (C_4)	180	3

The ranking procedure is accomplished on the ordinal

scale from 1 (high) to 4 (low). The formula designed
to determine the percentile rank[11] or weight, W_{Ci}, is

$$W_{Ci} = 100 - \frac{(100R - 50)}{N} ,$$

where R is the ranked score and N is the number of criteria that are ranked.

To determine the percentile rank (W_{Ci}) for distance
we substitute our data as follows:

$$W_{C1} = 100 - \frac{(100 (1) - 50)}{4} ,$$

$$= 100 - 12.5,$$

$$= 87.5.$$

Through the same procedure we are now able to determine the weights per criteria as shown below:

Criteria	W_{Ci}
Distance (C_1)	87.5
Availability (C_2)	12.5
Population (C_3)	62.5
Accessibility (C_4)	37.5

Now that the four major categories have been weighted
the next step involves a careful analysis of the components included in each criterion. Distance will be defined as the average distance from any two towns (in our
example) to the third town. For example, if the new
facility is located at Town A, then the average distance
from B and C to A is (7 + 6) ÷ 2 = 6.5 miles. However,
if the site were to be located in Town B, the distance
would be (7 + 5) ÷ 2 = 6 miles, or if the location were
at Town C, the distance would be (6 + 5) ÷ 2 = 5.5
miles. The distance criterion, C_{1j}, is now weighted for
each site (j = sites A, B, and C).

Site	Distance (miles)	Rank (R)
A	6.5	3
B	6.0	2
C	5.5	1

Thus, the average distance from the two remaining population centers serves as a score where the smaller number of miles ranks highest, while the greater distance
receives the lowest rank (1 is high and 3 is low). The

weight for distance is written symbolically as C_{1j} and for Town A we note that

$$C_{1A} = 100 - \frac{(100(3) - 50)}{3},$$

$$= 16.67.$$

Hence,

Site	Weight C_{1j}
A, C_{1A}	16.67
B, C_{1B}	50.00
C, C_{1C}	83.33

Assume that <u>availability</u>, C_2 or the second criterion, consists of the components below. For each site A, B, or C an "x" reveals whether or not the specific component is available at the designated location. The results of a survey are shown in the columns entitled "score" and "site," while the weight per site is denoted by C_{2j}.

		Site		
Availability	Score	A	B	C
Adequate land area	210	x	x	x
Public Library	96	x		
Gymnasium	84	x	x	
Soccer fields	72	x	x	x
Baseball fields	66		x	x
Tennis courts	52	x	x	x
Football field	47	x		x
Pool	38	x	x	x
Public Park	27		x	
Lake	15		x	
Total Score		599	564	485
Rank		1	2	3
Percentile rank (C_{2j})		83.33	50.00	16.67

Perhaps the only one of the above components that should be eliminated from the scoring procedure would be "adequate land area." In order for a town to be considered, it was understood that adequate land would be available. The cost of land is not included in this example but we shall include this variable in Problem 6.6.

Next, the criterion <u>population</u>, C_3, will be considered. Based on the expected student population 20

years into the future, the appropriate calculations for
our site selection model are as follows:

Town	Population	Rank	Percentile Rank
A	2,100	1	83.33
B	1,200	3	16.67
C	1,320	2	50.00

Here we note that population size is treated as a score
before the ranking.

Accessibility, C_4, is determined according to the
number of available highways where the following scores
are applied:

```
Interstate (I)        = 4 points
US Highway (US)       = 3 points
State Highway (SH)    = 2 points
County Highway (CH)   = 1 point
```

Thus, each town is evaluated as shown below:

Component	Number of Routes per Town		
	A	B	C
(I) 4	1		1
(US) 3		2	
(SH) 2	1	1	1
(CH) 1	2	3	2
Total Score	8	11	8
Rank	2.5	1	2.5
Percentile Rank or C_{4j}	33.33	83.33	33.33

A summary of the percentile ranks per town is shown
in Table 6.1. Based on the suitability score, S_j, of
each town, we shall now illustrate the best solution:

$$S_j = \frac{87.5 \, C_{1j} + 12.5 \, C_{2j} + 62.5 \, C_{3j} + 37.5 \, C_{4j}}{(87.5 + 12.5 + 62.5 + 37.5)}.$$

By substituting the data shown in Table 6.1 the results
for Town A are:

$$S_A = \frac{87.5(16.67) + 12.5(83.33) + 62.5(83.33) + 37.5(33.33),}{200}$$

$$S_A = \frac{1458.6 + 1041.6 + 5208.1 + 1249.9}{200},$$

$$= \frac{8958.2}{200},$$

$$= 44.8.$$

Next, the suitability of Town B, S_B, is determined.

$$S_B = \frac{87.5(50.00) + 12.5(50.00) + 62.5(16.67) + 37.5(83.33)}{200},$$

$$= \frac{4375 + 625 + 1041.9 + 3124.9}{200},$$

$$= \frac{9166.8}{200},$$

$$= 45.8.$$

Finally, the suitability for Town C, S_C, is calculated.

$$S_C = \frac{87.5(83.33) + 12.5(16.67) + 62.5(50.00) + 37.5(33.3)}{200},$$

$$= \frac{7291.4 + 208.4 + 3125 + 1249.9}{200},$$

$$= \frac{11874.7}{200},$$

$$= 59.4$$

Based on our comprehensive analysis through the modified land use screening procedure for siting, we find that Town C should be selected for the new facility. Solutions may be altered if new variables are

Table 6.1.   Summary of Percentile Ranks per
             Criterion for Problem 6.5

Criterion	W_{Ci}	Percentile Rank per Town		
		A	B	C
Distance	87.5	16.67	50.00	83.33
Availability	12.5	83.33	50.00	16.67
Population	62.5	83.33	16.67	50.00
Accessibility	37.5	33.33	83.33	33.33

introduced. The planner should take care regarding
how the scores are obtained, since variation at that
point can determine different results. Good data based
on sound research methods is indeed a must.

Now that one solution has been illustrated let us
determine a general formula for the model.

$$S_j = \frac{W_{C1}C_{1j} + W_{C2}C_{2j} + W_{C3}C_{3j} + W_{C4}C_{4j}}{(W_{C1} + W_{C2} + W_{C3} + W_{C4})} \quad ,$$

where $j = A, B, C$; C_{ij} $(i = 1,2,3,4)$ is the percentile
rank for the criteria per town, and W_{Ci} is the weight
per major criterion. Therefore the general formula for
the model is

$$S_j = \frac{\sum_{i=1}^{n} W_{Ci}C_{ij}}{\sum_{i=1}^{n} W_{Ci}} \quad .$$

where $i = 1, \ldots, n$, $j = 1,2, \ldots, m$. The n represents
the number of major criterion sets (each set may have
a different number of components), and m is the number
of towns or population centers. Thus W_{Ci} is the major
criterion weight, and C_{ij} is the weight for the criterion per population center. S_j represents the suitability for Town J.

THE MICROCOMPUTER'S SOLUTION TO A LAND USE SCREENING
PROBLEM

The microcomputer solution to Problem 6.5 is illustrated below. Perhaps the best approach would be to
convert the percentiles in Table 6.1 to ranks as illustrated in Table 6.2. Refer to Table 6.2, and note the
following interactions:

```
        RUN LAND USE SCREENING PROC


        INPUT NUMBER OF SITES TO BE CONSIDERED:
        ?3


        ENTER NAME OF SITE 1
        ?ALPHA

        ENTER NAME OF SITE 2
        ?BETA

        ENTER NAME OF SITE 3
        ?GAMMA

        ENTER NUMBER OF CRITERIA TO BE USED:
        ?4
```

```
ENTER NAME OF CRITERION 1
?DISTANCE

ENTER NAME OF CRITERION 2
?AVAILABILITY

ENTER NAME OF CRITERION 3
?POPULATION

ENTER NAME OF CRITERION 4
?ACCESSIBILITY

ENTER RANK ON CRITERION DISTANCE FOR ALPHA
?3
ENTER RANK ON CRITERION AVAILABILITY FOR ALPHA
?1
ENTER RANK ON CRITERION POPULATION FOR ALPHA
?1
ENTER RANK ON CRITERION ACCESSIBILITY FOR ALPHA
?2.5
ENTER RANK ON CRITERION DISTANCE FOR BETA
?2
ENTER RANK ON CRITERION AVAILABILITY FOR BETA
?2
ENTER RANK ON CRITERION POPULATION FOR BETA
?3
ENTER RANK ON CRITERION ACCESSIBILITY FOR BETA
?1
ENTER RANK ON CRITERION DISTANCE FOR GAMMA
?1
ENTER RANK ON CRITERION AVAILABILITY FOR GAMMA
?3
ENTER RANK ON CRITERION POPULATION FOR GAMMA
?2
ENTER RANK ON CRITERION ACCESSIBILITY FOR GAMMA

?2.5
ENTER RANK IN IMPORTANCE OF CRITERION DISTANCE
?1
ENTER RANK IN IMPORTANCE OF CRITERION AVAILABILITY
?4
ENTER RANK IN IMPORTANCE OF CRITERION POPULATION
?2
ENTER RANK IN IMPORTANCE OF CRITERION ACCESSIBILITY
?3
                PERCENTILE RANK PER TOWN
CRITERION      ALPHA    BETA    GAMMA
DISTANCE       16.6     50      83.3
AVAILABILITY   83.3     50      16.6
POPULATION     83.3     16.6    50
ACCESSIBILITY  33.3     83.3    33.3


SITE                SUITABILITY
----                -----------

ALPHA               44.7916667
BETA                45.8333334
GAMMA               59.375
```

Table 6.2.   Summary of Ranks per Criterion
             for Problem 6.5

Criterion	W_{Ci}*	Rank per Town		
		Alpha	Beta	Gamma
Distance	1	3	2	1
Availability	4	1	2	3
Population	2	1	3	2
Accessibility	3	2.5	1	2.5

*Rank of importance

Problem 6.6.   Assume that we have the same problem as presented in Problem 6.5, but with cost as the additional variable.

Criteria	Score	Rank
Distance (C_1)	275	2
Availability (C_2)	175	5
Population (C_3)	215	3
Accessibility (C_4)	180	4
Cost of Land (C_5)	320	1

Solution.   The problem may be solved as follows:

$$W_{C1} = 100 - \frac{(100(2) - 50)}{5} ,$$

$$= 70.$$

Substituting each rank consecutively, we find that

$$W_{C2} = 10, \quad W_{C3} = 50, \quad W_{C4} = 30, \quad \text{and} \quad W_{C5} = 90.$$

Thus at this point the formula

$$S_j = \frac{70C_{1j} + 10C_{2j} + 50C_{3j} + 30C_{4j} + 90C_{5j}}{(70 + 10 + 50 + 30 + 90)} .$$

Since the first four sets of C_{ij} have been determined previously we only need to calculate C_{5j}.   Therefore, we obtain the cost data for the required land site (300 acres per site).

Site	Cost
A	$1,500,000
B	1,400,000
C	1,650,000

Since we wish to minimize cost, the property with the lowest price, all other things equal, would receive the best rank. Hence,

Site	Rank	C_{5j}
A	2	50.00
B	1	83.33
C	3	16.67

Table 6.3 reveals the weights per major criterion and each population center, A, B, and C.   The suitability score for A is:

$$S_A = \frac{70(16.67)+10(83.33)+50(83.33)+30(33.33)+90(50.00),}{70 + 10 + 50 + 30 + 90}$$

$$= \frac{1166.9 + 833.3 + 4166.5 + 999.9 + 4500}{250},$$

$$= \frac{11666.6}{250},$$

$$= 46.7.$$

By continuing the process for B and C we find $S_B = 59.3$, and $S_C = 44.0$. Thus, the cost of land influenced the suitability score such that site B is selected, although in Problem 6.5 we found that site C was the best choice. This is not an unrealistic solution since the difference in the cost of money would be a significant factor if $150,000 or $100,000 were financed over a 10- to 20-year period.

THE SITE SELECTION AND DEVELOPMENT PROCESS

Before utilizing the site selection models presented in the previous sections, the planner should understand where the site selection and development process fits into the total planning scheme. Obviously it is wise to know the program goals and objectives and to obtain good data relevant to expected population trends and financial abilities of the communities or districts desiring new facilities. Brooks, Conrad, and Griffith[12] have developed a comprehensive approach to site selection and facilities planning. Siting and facilities planning guidelines are also offered by the Council of Educational Facilities Planners, International.[13]

Table 6.3. Percentile Ranks W_{Ci} and C_{ij} for Problem 6.6

Criterion	W_{Ci}	A	B	C
Distance	70	16.67	50.00	83.33
Availability	10	83.33	50.00	16.67
Population	50	83.33	16.67	50.00
Accessibility	30	33.33	83.33	33.33
Cost of Land	90	50.00	83.33	16.67

The initial step in site selection involves the nomination and appointment of a team to be responsible for recommending an appropriate site. Some of the location criteria that this group should consider are

1. Functions of the programs to be offered in the new facility
2. Philosophy goals and objectives of the program
3. Financial ability of the district and state
4. Environmental impacts
5. Costs of alternative sites
6. Site development costs
7. Possible expansion in the future
8. Energy costs for each alternative site
9. Transportation costs from various population centers to each alternative site.

The above set of criteria may be expanded as careful study is given to the total need. Once the criteria have been identified, application of one of the models presented in this chapter is appropriate. This process will help narrow the choices among alternatives. The final phase of the selection process may involve the approval by a state agency or local school board before the purchase of a given site.

SUMMARY

Three planning models were presented in this chapter. One boundary selection model and two site location models were discussed. The planner was exposed to these rational systems models through the use of examples and problems. Emphasis was placed on quantitative data for decisions among alternatives; however, special attention was given to subjective information and politics. Awareness of the total situation is an underlying assumption of all planning models discussed in this text. Additional problems regarding concepts in this chapter are presented in Appendix B. Microcomputer programs for solving these problems are presented in Appendix A.

Appendices
Notes
About the Authors
Index

Appendix A
Microcomputer
Program

A microcomputer program is presented in this section. It is written in BASIC for the Apple computer
systems. The program consists of the following parts:
CPM, PERT, Stand Compound Interest Model, Total Housing Units, Payback Schedule, Grade Progression Ratio
Model, Linear Regression Model, Bayesian Forecast,
Facility Requirements, Breaking Point Model, and Land
Use Screening Proc. Only minor changes are needed to
adapt the program to other computer systems. As explained in the Introduction, the programs are available
from the authors on diskette for the Apple system.

```
]LIST

1000   HOME
1005   DIM A(70),B(70),C(70),D(70),E(70),F(70),G(70),H(70)
1010   DIM I(10),J(10),K(10),L(10),M(4),N(4),P(5),Q(5),R(4),S(10),T(4),U(4)
       ,V(4),W(4)
1015   DIM X(70),Y(70),Z(70)
1020   DIM PY(70),VS(70),XS(70),XY(70),YS(70)
1025   DIM A$(10),B$(10)
1030   DIM CC(25,25),DD(25,25),KK(25,25)
1035   DIM TE(70)
1040   CALL  - 936: PRINT : PRINT : PRINT "  1 = CPM": PRINT : PRINT "  2
       = PERT"
1045   PRINT : PRINT "  3 = STAND COMPOUND INTEREST MODEL"
1050   PRINT : PRINT "  4 = TOTAL HOUSING UNITS"
1055   PRINT : PRINT "  5 = PAYBACK SCHEDULE"
1060   PRINT : PRINT "  6 = GRADE PROGRESSION RATIO MODEL"
1065   PRINT : PRINT "  7 = LINEAR REGRESSION MODEL"
1070   PRINT : PRINT "  8 = BAYESIAN FORECAST"
1075   PRINT : PRINT "  9 = FACILITY REQUIREMENTS"
1080   PRINT : PRINT " 10 = BREAKING POINT MODEL": PRINT : PRINT " 11 = LA
       ND USE SCREENING PROC"
```

```
1085   PRINT : PRINT " 12 = END"
1090   INPUT "Select one: ";ZA
1095   IF ZA = 1 GOTO 1155
1100   IF ZA = 2 GOTO 1395
1105   IF ZA = 3 GOTO 1755
1110   IF ZA = 4 GOTO 1960
1115   IF ZA = 5 GOTO 2165
1120   IF ZA = 6 GOTO 2575
1125   IF ZA = 7 GOTO 4065
1130   IF ZA = 8 GOTO 4700
1135   IF ZA = 9 GOTO 5065
1140   IF ZA = 10 GOTO 5285
1145   IF ZA = 11 GOTO 5405
1150   IF ZA = 12 GOTO 5795
1155   CALL  - 936
1160   PRINT "CPM"
1165   PRINT : PRINT : PRINT : PRINT : PRINT
1170   PRINT "LABEL EACH ACTIVITY WITH A NUMBER"
1175   PRINT
1180   PRINT "INPUT THE NUMBER OF ACTIVITIES ON THE ACTIVITY NETWORK."
1185   INPUT Z
1190   CALL  - 936
1195   PRINT
1200   FOR S1 = 1 TO Z
1205   PRINT "ENTER TIME FOR ACTIVITY "S1
1210   INPUT C(S1)
1215   NEXT S1
1220   CALL  - 936
1225   INPUT "Enter the number of paths: ";F
1230   PRINT
1235   FOR I = 1 TO F
1240   PRINT "Enter the number of activities which lie along path "I
1245   INPUT H(I)
1250   PRINT
1255   PRINT "Enter the activities, by number, which lie along path "I
1260   FOR S = 1 TO H(I)
1265   INPUT D(S)
1270   NEXT S
1275   CALL  - 936
1280 Z(I) = 0
1285   FOR S = 1 TO H(I)
1290 Z(I) = Z(I) + C(D(S))
1295   NEXT S
1300   CALL  - 936
1305   NEXT I
1310 TV = 0: CALL  - 936
1315   CALL  - 936
1320 I = 0
1325 I = I + 1
1330 S = 0
1335 S = S + 1
1340   IF S > F GOTO 1360
1345   IF Z(I) < Z(S) GOTO 1325
1350   GOTO 1335
```

```
1360    PRINT "Path "I" is the critical path."
1365    PRINT : PRINT : PRINT : PRINT
1370    PRINT "Length of critical path = "Z(I)
1375    PRINT : PRINT : PRINT : PRINT : PRINT "RETURN TO GO BACK TO MENU"
1380    INPUT ZB$
1385    IF ZB$ = "" GOTO 1040
1395    CALL  - 936
1405    PRINT "PERT"
1410    PRINT : PRINT : PRINT : PRINT
1415    PRINT "After labeling each activity on the PERT"
1420    PRINT "Chart with a number, label each with"
1425    PRINT "the most optimistic, the most likely,"
1430    PRINT "and the most pessimistic time for"
1435    PRINT "completion."
1440    PRINT
1445    PRINT "INPUT THE NUMBER OF ACTIVITIES ON THE   PERT CHART."
1450    INPUT Z
1455    CALL  - 936
1460    PRINT "Beginning with ACTIVITY 1 and continuing"
1465    PRINT "in numerical order, enter first the most"
1470    PRINT "optimistic, then the most likely, and"
1475    PRINT "finally the most pessimistic time for"
1480    PRINT "completion for each activity."
1485    PRINT
1490    FOR S1 = 1 TO Z
1495    PRINT "ENTER TIMES FOR ACTIVITY "S1
1500    INPUT A(S1)
1505    INPUT C(S1)
1510    INPUT B(S1)
1515    NEXT S1
1520    FOR S1 = 1 TO Z
1525 TE(S1) = (A(S1) + (4 * C(S1)) + B(S1)) / 6
1530 X(S1) = (B(S1) - A(S1)) / 6
1535 VS(S1) = X(S1) * X(S1)
1540    NEXT S1
1545    CALL  - 936
1550    INPUT "Input the number of paths: ";F
1555    PRINT : FOR I = 1 TO F
1560    PRINT "Enter the number of activities which lie on path "I
1565    INPUT H(I)
1570    PRINT
1575    PRINT "Enter the activities, by number, which lie along path "I
1580    FOR S = 1 TO H(I)
1585    INPUT DD(I,S)
1590    NEXT S
1595    CALL  - 936
1600 Z(I) = 0
1605    FOR S = 1 TO H(I)
1610 Z(I) = Z(I) + TE(DD(I,S))
1615    NEXT S
1620    NEXT I
1625    CALL  - 936
1630    PRINT "ENTER TIME ALLOWED FOR COMPLETION OF THE PROJECT."
1635    INPUT TT
```

```
1640 TV = 0: CALL  - 936
1645 I = 0
1650 I = I + 1
1655 S = 0
1660 S = S + 1
1665  IF S > F GOTO 1685
1670  IF Z(I) < Z(S) GOTO 1650
1675  GOTO 1660
1685  FOR S = 1 TO H(I)
1690 TV = TV + VS(DD(I,S))
1695  NEXT S
1700 TR = TV ^ .5
1705 ZZ = (TT - Z(I)) / TR
1710  PRINT "Path "I" is the critical path."
1715  PRINT : PRINT : PRINT : PRINT
1720  PRINT "WEIGHTED TIME ESTIMATE = ";Z(I)
1725  PRINT : PRINT : PRINT : PRINT "Z FOR COMPLETION IN ";TT;" UNITS OF
     TIME = ";ZZ
1735  PRINT : PRINT : PRINT : PRINT : PRINT "RETURN TO GO BACK TO MENU"
1740  INPUT ZB$
1745  IF ZB$ = "" GOTO 1040
1755  CALL  - 936
1770  PRINT "STAND COMPOUND INTEREST MODEL"
1775  PRINT : PRINT : PRINT : PRINT
1780  PRINT "NUMBER OF TIME PERIODS FOR WHICH DATA   ARE AVAILABLE:"
1785  INPUT Y
1790  PRINT " LENGTH OF TIME PERIOD IN YEARS:"
1795  INPUT C
1800  PRINT "BEGINNING WITH OLDEST DATA, ENTER DATA  CONSECUTIVELY:"
1805  FOR S1 = 1 TO Y + 1
1810  INPUT A(S1)
1815  NEXT S1
1820  FOR S1 = 1 TO Y
1825 B(S1) = (A(S1 + 1) - A(S1)) / A(S1)
1830  NEXT S1
1835  LET T1 = 0
1840  FOR S1 = 1 TO Y
1845  LET T1 = T1 + B(S1)
1850  NEXT S1
1855 R = T1 / Y
1860 R1 = R + 1
1865  FOR S1 = 1 TO Y + 1
1870 PY(S1) = A(Y + 1) * (R1 ^ S1)
1875  NEXT S1
1880  CALL  - 936
1885  GOSUB 1915
1890  PRINT : PRINT : PRINT : PRINT : PRINT
1895  FOR S1 = 1 TO Y + 1
1900  PRINT "PY"S1 * C; TAB( 10);PY(S1)
1905  NEXT S1
1910  GOTO 1940
1915  FOR S1 = 1 TO Y + 1
1920 PY(S1) =  INT (PY(S1) + .5)
1925  NEXT S1
```

```
1930   RETURN
1935   HOME
1940   PRINT : PRINT : PRINT : PRINT : PRINT "RETURN TO GO BACK TO MENU"
1945   INPUT ZB$
1950   IF ZB$ = "" GOTO 1040
1960   HOME
1965   PRINT "TOTAL HOUSING UNITS"
1970   PRINT : PRINT : PRINT : PRINT : PRINT
1980   PRINT "Enter the number of time periods for"
1985   PRINT "which forecasts of the number of"
1990   PRINT "households are available:"
1995   INPUT N1
2000   PRINT : PRINT "Enter the length of the time periods:"
2005   INPUT N2
2010   HOME
2015   PRINT "Enter the rate of dilapidation:"
2020   INPUT D
2025   HOME
2030   PRINT "Enter the number of households at"
2035   PRINT "present:"
2040   INPUT A(1)
2045   PRINT : PRINT : PRINT "Beginning with PY"N2", enter forecasts"
2050   PRINT "of households:"
2055   FOR I = 1 TO N1
2060   INPUT A(I + 1)
2065   NEXT I
2070   FOR I = 1 TO N1
2075 B(I) = A(I + 1) - A(I)
2080   NEXT I
2085 E(1) = A(1) * D
2090   FOR I = 2 TO N1
2095 E(I) = E(I - 1) - (D * E(I - 1))
2100   NEXT I
2105   FOR I = 1 TO N1
2110 C(I) = E(I) + B(I)
2115   NEXT I
2120   HOME
2125   PRINT "PLANNING YEAR     NEW UNITS REQUIRED"
2130   FOR I = 1 TO N1
2135   PRINT "    PY"N2 * I"                 "C(I)
2140   NEXT I
2145   PRINT : PRINT : PRINT : PRINT : PRINT : PRINT
2150   PRINT "RETURN TO GO BACK TO MENU"
2155   INPUT ZB$
2160   IF ZB$ = "" GOTO 1040
2165   CALL  - 936
2175   PRINT "PAYBACK SCHEDULE"
2180   PRINT : PRINT : PRINT : PRINT : PRINT
2185   PRINT "ENTER AMOUNT FINANCED."
2190   INPUT R1
2195   PRINT : PRINT "ENTER INTEREST RATE."
2200   INPUT R2
2205   PRINT : PRINT "ENTER NUMBER OF YEARS OF PAYBACK."
2210   INPUT R3
```

```
2215   PRINT : PRINT "ENTER YEAR IN WHICH 1ST PAYMENT ON PRINCIPAL
       IS TO BE MADE."
2220   INPUT R4
2230   FOR S1 = 1 TO R3
2235  A(S1) = S1
2240   NEXT S1
2250  R5 = (R3 - R4) + 1
2255  R6 = R1 / R5
2260  R6 =   INT (R6 + .5)
2270   FOR S1 = R4 TO R3
2275  B(S1) = R6
2280   NEXT S1
2290  TB = 0
2295   FOR S1 = 1 TO R3
2300  TB = TB + B(S1)
2305   NEXT S1
2315  E(0) = R1
2320   FOR S1 = 1 TO R3
2325  E(S1) = E(S1 - 1) - B(S1)
2330   NEXT S1
2340   FOR S1 = 1 TO R3
2345  C(S1) = ((R2 + 1) - 1) * E(S1 - 1)
2350   NEXT S1
2360  TC = 0
2365   FOR S1 = 1 TO R3
2370  C(S1) =   INT (C(S1) + .5)
2375   NEXT S1
2385   FOR S1 = 1 TO R3
2390  TC = TC + C(S1)
2395   NEXT S1
2405   FOR S1 = 1 TO R3
2410  D(S1) = B(S1) + C(S1)
2415   NEXT S1
2425  TD = 0
2430   FOR S1 = 1 TO R3
2435  TD = TD + D(S1)
2440   NEXT S1
2450   CALL  - 936
2455   PRINT : PRINT : PRINT : PRINT : PRINT
2460   PRINT "YEAR"; TAB( 6);"PRINCIPAL"; TAB( 17);"INTEREST"; TAB( 27);
      "TOTAL"
2465   PRINT
2470   FOR S1 = 1 TO R3
2475   PRINT " PY"A(S1); TAB( 7);B(S1); TAB( 17);C(S1); TAB( 27);D(S1)
2480   NEXT S1
2485   PRINT   TAB( 7);"-------"; TAB( 17);"-------"; TAB( 27);"--------"
2490   PRINT   TAB( 7);TB; TAB( 17);TC; TAB( 27);TD
2500   PRINT : PRINT : PRINT : PRINT
2505   PRINT "RETURN TO DISPLAY 'BALANCE OF PRINCIPAL' DATA."
2510   INPUT S$
2515   PRINT : PRINT : PRINT : PRINT : PRINT
2520   IF S$ = "" GOTO 2525
2525   CALL  - 936
2535   PRINT "YEAR"; TAB( 6);"BALANCE OF PRINCIPAL"
```

```
2540   PRINT : FOR S1 = 1 TO R3
2545   PRINT  TAB( 2);"PY"A(S1); TAB( 7);E(S1)
2550   NEXT S1
2555   PRINT : PRINT : PRINT : PRINT : PRINT "RETURN TO GO BACK TO MENU"
2560   INPUT ZB$
2565   IF ZB$ = "" GOTO 1040
2575   CALL  - 936
2580   PRINT "GRADE PROGRESSION RATIO MODEL"
2585   PRINT : PRINT : PRINT : PRINT
2595   PRINT "ENTER RESIDENT LIVE BIRTH DATA FOR LAST TEN YEARS"
2600   PRINT "    BEGINNING WITH OLDEST DATA"
2605   FOR S1 = 1 TO 10
2610   INPUT X(S1)
2615   NEXT S1
2620   CALL  - 936
2625   PRINT "ENTER ENROLLMENT DATA FOR FOUR YEARS AGO BEGINNING WITH GRAD
       E ONE"
2630   INPUT A(1)
2635   INPUT B(1)
2640   INPUT C(1)
2645   INPUT D(1)
2650   INPUT E(1)
2655   INPUT F(1)
2660   INPUT G(1)
2665   INPUT H(1)
2670   INPUT I(1)
2675   INPUT J(1)
2680   INPUT K(1)
2685   INPUT L(1)
2690   PRINT "ENTER ENROLLMENT DATA FOR THREE YEARS AGO BEGINNING WITH GRA
       DE ONE"
2695   INPUT A(2)
2700   INPUT B(2)
2705   INPUT C(2)
2710   INPUT D(2)
2715   INPUT E(2)
2720   INPUT F(2)
2725   INPUT G(2)
2730   INPUT H(2)
2735   INPUT I(2)
2740   INPUT J(2)
2745   INPUT K(2)
2750   INPUT L(2)
2755   PRINT "ENTER ENROLLMENT DATA FOR TWO YEARS AGO BEGINNING WITH GRADE
       ONE"
2760   INPUT A(3)
2765   INPUT B(3)
2770   INPUT C(3)
2775   INPUT D(3)
2780   INPUT E(3)
2785   INPUT F(3)
2790   INPUT G(3)
2795   INPUT H(3)
2800   INPUT I(3)
```

```
2805    INPUT J(3)
2810    INPUT K(3)
2815    INPUT L(3)
2820    PRINT "ENTER LAST YEAR'S ENROLLMENT DATA BEGINNING WITH GRADE ONE"
2825    INPUT A(4)
2830    INPUT B(4)
2835    INPUT C(4)
2840    INPUT D(4)
2845    INPUT E(4)
2850    INPUT F(4)
2855    INPUT G(4)
2860    INPUT H(4)
2865    INPUT I(4)
2870    INPUT J(4)
2875    INPUT K(4)
2880    INPUT L(4)
2885    PRINT "ENTER THIS YEAR'S ENROLLMENT DATA BEGINNING WITH GRADE ONE"
2890    INPUT A(5)
2895    INPUT B(5)
2900    INPUT C(5)
2905    INPUT D(5)
2910    INPUT E(5)
2915    INPUT F(5)
2920    INPUT G(5)
2925    INPUT H(5)
2930    INPUT I(5)
2935    INPUT J(5)
2940    INPUT K(5)
2945    INPUT L(5)
2950    FOR S1 = 1 TO 5
2955 P(S1) = A(S1) / X(S1)
2960    NEXT S1
2965 T1 = 0
2970    FOR S1 = 1 TO 5
2975 T1 = T1 + P(S1)
2980    NEXT S1
2985 T1 = T1 / 5
2994 S1 = 0
2995 S1 = S1 + 1
2996    ONERR  GOTO 6500
2997    IF S1 > 4 GOTO 3010
3000 Q(S1) = B(S1 + 1) / A(S1)
3005    GOTO 2995
3010 T2 = 0
3014 S1 = 0
3015 S1 = S1 + 1
3017    IF S1 > 4 GOTO 3030
3020 T2 = T2 + Q(S1)
3025    GOTO 3015
3030 T2 = T2 / 4
3039 S1 = 0
3040 S1 = S1 + 1
3041    ONERR  GOTO 6450
3042    IF S1 > 4 GOTO 3055
```

```
3045  LET R(S1) = C(S1 + 1) / B(S1)
3050  GOTO 3040
3055 T3 = 0
3059 S1 = 0
3060 S1 = S1 + 1
3062  IF S1 > 4 GOTO 3075
3065 T3 = T3 + R(S1)
3070  GOTO 3060
3075 T3 = T3 / 4
3084 S1 = 0
3085 S1 = S1 + 1
3086  ONERR  GOTO 6400
3087  IF S1 > 4 GOTO 3100
3090  LET S(S1) = D(S1 + 1) / C(S1)
3095  GOTO 3085
3100 T4 = 0
3104 S1 = 0
3105 S1 = S1 + 1
3107  IF S1 > 4 GOTO 3120
3110 T4 = T4 + S(S1)
3115  GOTO 3105
3120 T4 = T4 / 4
3129 S1 = 0
3130 S1 = S1 + 1
3131  ONERR  GOTO 6350
3132  IF S1 > 4 GOTO 3145
3135  LET T(S1) = E(S1 + 1) / D(S1)
3140  GOTO 3130
3145 T5 = 0
3149 S1 = 0
3150 S1 = S1 + 1
3152  IF S1 > 4 GOTO 3165
3155 T5 = T5 + T(S1)
3160  GOTO 3150
3165 T5 = T5 / 4
3174 S1 = 0
3175 S1 = S1 + 1
3176  ONERR  GOTO 6300
3177  IF S1 > 4 GOTO 3190
3180  LET U(S1) = F(S1 + 1) / E(S1)
3185  GOTO 3175
3190 T6 = 0
3194 S1 = 0
3195 S1 = S1 + 1
3197  IF S1 > 4 GOTO 3210
3200 T6 = T6 + U(S1)
3205  GOTO 3195
3210 T6 = T6 / 4
3219 S1 = 0
3220 S1 = S1 + 1
3221  ONERR  GOTO 6250
3222  IF S1 > 4 GOTO 3235
3225  LET V(S1) = G(S1 + 1) / F(S1)
3230  GOTO 3220
```

```
3235 T7 = 0
3239 S1 = 0
3240 S1 = S1 + 1
3242  IF S1 > 4 GOTO 3255
3245 T7 = T7 + V(S1)
3250  GOTO 3240
3255 T7 = T7 / 4
3264 S1 = 0
3265 S1 = S1 + 1
3266  ONERR  GOTO 6200
3267  IF S1 > 4 GOTO 3280
3270  LET W(S1) = H(S1 + 1) / G(S1)
3275  GOTO 3265
3280 T8 = 0
3284 S1 = 0
3285 S1 = S1 + 1
3287  IF S1 > 4 GOTO 3300
3290 T8 = T8 + W(S1)
3295  GOTO 3285
3300 T8 = T8 / 4
3309 S1 = 0
3310 S1 = S1 + 1
3311  ONERR  GOTO 6000
3312  IF S1 > 4 GOTO 3325
3315  LET Y(S1) = I(S1 + 1) / H(S1)
3320  GOTO 3310
3325 T9 = 0
3329 S1 = 0
3330 S1 = S1 + 1
3332  IF S1 > 4 GOTO 3345
3335 T9 = T9 + Y(S1)
3340  GOTO 3330
3345 T9 = T9 / 4
3354 S1 = 0
3355 S1 = S1 + 1
3356  ONERR  GOTO 6050
3357  IF S1 > 4 GOTO 3370
3360  LET Z(S1) = J(S1 + 1) / I(S1)
3365  GOTO 3355
3370 U1 = 0
3374 S1 = 0
3375 S1 = S1 + 1
3377  IF S1 > 4 GOTO 3390
3380 U1 = U1 + Z(S1)
3385  GOTO 3375
3390 U1 = U1 / 4
3399 S1 = 0
3400 S1 = S1 + 1
3401  ONERR  GOTO 6100
3402  IF S1 > 4 GOTO 3415
3405  LET M(S1) = K(S1 + 1) / J(S1)
3410  GOTO 3400
3415 U2 = 0
3419 S1 = 0
```

```
3420 S1 = S1 + 1
3422  IF S1 > 4 GOTO 3435
3425 U2 = U2 + M(S1)
3430  GOTO 3420
3435 U2 = U2 / 4
3440 S1 = 0
3445 S1 = S1 + 1
3446  ONERR  GOTO 6150
3447  IF S1 > 4 GOTO 3460
3450  LET N(S1) = L(S1 + 1) / K(S1)
3455  GOTO 3445
3460 U3 = 0
3464 S1 = 0
3465 S1 = S1 + 1
3466  IF S1 > 4 GOTO 3480
3470 U3 = U3 + N(S1)
3475  GOTO 3465
3480 U3 = U3 / 4
3485  FOR S1 = 1 TO 5
3490 A(S1 + 5) = T1 * X(S1 + 5)
3495  NEXT S1
3505  FOR S1 = 1 TO 5
3510 B(S1 + 5) = T2 * A(S1 + 4)
3515  NEXT S1
3525  FOR S1 = 1 TO 5
3530 C(S1 + 5) = T3 * B(S1 + 4)
3535  NEXT S1
3545  FOR S1 = 1 TO 5
3550 D(S1 + 5) = T4 * C(S1 + 4)
3555  NEXT S1
3565  FOR S1 = 1 TO 5
3570 E(S1 + 5) = T5 * D(S1 + 4)
3575  NEXT S1
3585  FOR S1 = 1 TO 5
3590 F(S1 + 5) = T6 * E(S1 + 4)
3595  NEXT S1
3605  FOR S1 = 1 TO 5
3610 G(S1 + 5) = T7 * F(S1 + 4)
3615  NEXT S1
3625  FOR S1 = 1 TO 5
3630 H(S1 + 5) = T8 * G(S1 + 4)
3635  NEXT S1
3645  FOR S1 = 1 TO 5
3650 I(S1 + 5) = T9 * H(S1 + 4)
3655  NEXT S1
3665  FOR S1 = 1 TO 5
3670 J(S1 + 5) = U1 * I(S1 + 4)
3675  NEXT S1
3685  FOR S1 = 1 TO 5
3690 K(S1 + 5) = U2 * J(S1 + 4)
3695  NEXT S1
3705  FOR S1 = 1 TO 5
3710 L(S1 + 5) = U3 * K(S1 + 4)
3715  NEXT S1
```

```
3725  FOR S1 = 1 TO 5
3730  A(S1 + 5) =  INT (A(S1 + 5) + .5)
3735  NEXT S1
3745  FOR S1 = 1 TO 5
3750  B(S1 + 5) =  INT (B(S1 + 5) + .5)
3755  NEXT S1
3765  FOR S1 = 1 TO 5
3770  C(S1 + 5) =  INT (C(S1 + 5) + .5)
3775  NEXT S1
3785  FOR S1 = 1 TO 5
3790  D(S1 + 5) =  INT (D(S1 + 5) + .5)
3795  NEXT S1
3805  FOR S1 = 1 TO 5
3810  E(S1 + 5) =  INT (E(S1 + 5) + .5)
3815  NEXT S1
3825  FOR S1 = 1 TO 5
3830  F(S1 + 5) =  INT (F(S1 + 5) + .5)
3835  NEXT S1
3845  FOR S1 = 1 TO 5
3850  G(S1 + 5) =  INT (G(S1 + 5) + .5)
3855  NEXT S1
3865  FOR S1 = 1 TO 5
3870  H(S1 + 5) =  INT (H(S1 + 5) + .5)
3875  NEXT S1
3885  FOR S1 = 1 TO 5
3890  I(S1 + 5) =  INT (I(S1 + 5) + .5)
3895  NEXT S1
3905  FOR S1 = 1 TO 5
3910  J(S1 + 5) =  INT (J(S1 + 5) + .5)
3915  NEXT S1
3925  FOR S1 = 1 TO 5
3930  K(S1 + 5) =  INT (K(S1 + 5) + .5)
3935  NEXT S1
3945  FOR S1 = 1 TO 5
3950  L(S1 + 5) =  INT (L(S1 + 5) + .5)
3955  NEXT S1
3965  CALL  - 936
3970  PRINT  TAB( 15);"FORECAST"
3975  PRINT : PRINT : PRINT
3980  PRINT "GRADE   PY1   PY2   PY3   PY4   PY5"
3985  PRINT  TAB( 3);"1"; TAB( 10);A(6); TAB( 16);A(7); TAB( 22);A(8);
      TAB( 28);A(9); TAB( 34);A(10)
3990  PRINT  TAB( 3);"2"; TAB( 10);B(6); TAB( 16);B(7); TAB( 22);B(8);
      TAB( 28);B(9); TAB( 34);B(10)
3995  PRINT  TAB( 3);"3"; TAB( 10);C(6); TAB( 16);C(7); TAB( 22);C(8);
      TAB( 28);C(9); TAB( 34);C(10)
4000  PRINT  TAB( 3);"4"; TAB( 10);D(6); TAB( 16);D(7); TAB( 22);D(8);
      TAB( 28);D(9); TAB( 34);D(10)
4005  PRINT  TAB( 3);"5"; TAB( 10);E(6); TAB( 16);E(7); TAB( 22);E(8);
      TAB( 28);E(9); TAB( 34);E(10)
4010  PRINT  TAB( 3);"6"; TAB( 10);F(6); TAB( 16);F(7); TAB( 22);F(8);
      TAB( 28);F(9); TAB( 34);F(10)
4015  PRINT  TAB( 3);"7"; TAB( 10);G(6); TAB( 16);G(7); TAB( 22);G(8);
      TAB( 28);G(9); TAB( 34);G(10)
```

```
4020   PRINT  TAB( 3);"8"; TAB( 10);H(6); TAB( 16);H(7); TAB( 22);H(8);
       TAB( 28);H(9); TAB( 34);H(10)
4025   PRINT  TAB( 3);"9"; TAB( 10);I(6); TAB( 16);I(7); TAB( 22);I(8);
       TAB( 28);I(9); TAB( 34);I(10)
4030   PRINT  TAB( 3);"10"; TAB( 10);J(6); TAB( 16);J(7); TAB( 22);J(8);
       TAB( 28);J(9); TAB( 34);J(10)
4035   PRINT  TAB( 3);"11"; TAB( 10);K(6); TAB( 16);K(7); TAB( 22);K(8);
       TAB( 28);K(9); TAB( 34);K(10)
4040   PRINT  TAB( 3);"12"; TAB( 10);L(6); TAB( 16);L(7); TAB( 22);L(8);
       TAB( 28);L(9); TAB( 34);L(10)
4045   PRINT : PRINT : PRINT : PRINT : PRINT "RETURN TO GO BACK TO MENU"
4050   INPUT ZB$
4055   IF ZB$ = "" GOTO 1040
4065   CALL  - 936
4075   PRINT "LINEAR REGRESSION MODEL"
4080   PRINT : PRINT : PRINT : PRINT
4085   PRINT "ENTER NUMBER OF YEARS OF AVAILABLE DATA"
4090   INPUT S2
4105   CALL  - 936
4120   FOR S1 = 1 TO 2 * S2
4125  X(S1) = S1
4130   NEXT S1
4145   PRINT "ENTER ENROLLMENT DATA FOR LAST "S2" YEARS BEGINNING WITH OLD
       EST DATA"
4150   FOR S1 = 1 TO S2
4155   INPUT Y(S1)
4160   NEXT S1
4175   FOR S1 = 1 TO S2
4180  XY(S1) = X(S1) * Y(S1)
4185   NEXT S1
4200   FOR S1 = 1 TO S2
4205  YS(S1) = Y(S1) * Y(S1)
4210   NEXT S1
4225   FOR S1 = 1 TO S2
4230  XS(S1) = X(S1) * X(S1)
4235   NEXT S1
4250  T1 = 0
4255   FOR S1 = 1 TO S2
4260  T1 = T1 + X(S1)
4265   NEXT S1
4280  T2 = 0
4285   FOR S1 = 1 TO S2
4290  T2 = T2 + Y(S1)
4295   NEXT S1
4310  T3 = 0
4315   FOR S1 = 1 TO S2
4320  T3 = T3 + XY(S1)
4325   NEXT S1
4340  T4 = 0
4345   FOR S1 = 1 TO S2
4350  T4 = T4 + XS(S1)
4355   NEXT S1
4370  T5 = 0
4375   FOR S1 = 1 TO S2
```

```
4380 T5 = T5 + YS(S1)
4385  NEXT S1
4400 MX = T1 / S2
4405 MY = T2 / S2
4420  FOR S1 = 1 TO S2
4425 Z(S1) = (Y(S1) - MY) * (Y(S1) - MY)
4430  NEXT S1
4445 T6 = 0
4450  FOR S1 = 1 TO S2
4455 T6 = T6 + Z(S1)
4460  NEXT S1
4475 B = ((S2 * T3) - (T1 * T2)) / ((S2 * T4) - (T1 * T1))
4490 A = MY - (MX * B)
4505  FOR S1 = (S2 + 1) TO (2 * S2)
4510 Y(S1) = A + (B * X(S1))
4515  NEXT S1
4530 SD = (T6 / S2) ^ .5
4545 R1 = ((S2 * T3) - (T1 * T2))
4550 R2 = ((S2 * T4) - (T1 * T1)) * ((S2 * T5) - (T2 * T2))
4555 RS = (R1 * R1) / R2
4570  ONERR  GOTO 4685
4575 R3 = 1 - RS
4580 R4 = R3 ^ .5
4585 SE = SD * R4
4600  FOR S1 = S2 + 1 TO 2 * S2
4605 Y(S1) =  INT (Y(S1) + .5)
4610  NEXT S1
4625  CALL  - 936
4630  PRINT : PRINT : PRINT : PRINT : PRINT
4635  PRINT "PY1"; TAB( 7);Y(S2 + 1); TAB( 15);"SE = "SE
4640  PRINT "PY2"; TAB( 7);Y(S2 + 2); TAB( 15);"SLOPE = "B
4645  PRINT "PY3"; TAB( 7);Y(S2 + 3); TAB( 15);"INTERCEPT = "A
4650  FOR S1 = 4 TO S2
4655  PRINT "PY"S1; TAB( 7);Y(S1 + S2)
4660  NEXT S1
4670  PRINT : PRINT : PRINT : PRINT : PRINT "RETURN TO GO BACK TO MENU"
4675  INPUT ZB$
4680  IF ZB$ = "" GOTO 1040
4685 SE = 0
4690  GOTO 4595
4700  CALL  - 936
4710  PRINT "BAYESIAN FORECAST"
4715  PRINT : PRINT : PRINT : PRINT
4720  PRINT "ENTER NUMBER OF YEARS OF AVAILABLE PREDICTIVE DATA"
4725  INPUT S2
4740  CALL  - 936
4745  PRINT "ENTER DATA FOR PY1 TO PY"S2" FROM GPR MODEL"
4750  FOR S1 = 1 TO S2
4755  INPUT G(S1)
4760  NEXT S1
4770  PRINT "ENTER DATA FOR PY1 TO PY"S2" FROM SCI MODEL"
4775  FOR S1 = 1 TO S2
4780  INPUT S(S1)
4785  NEXT S1
```

```
4795   PRINT "ENTER DATA FOR PY1 TO PY"S2"FROM LR MODEL"
4800   FOR S1 = 1 TO S2
4805   INPUT L(S1)
4810   NEXT S1
4825 T1 = 0
4830   FOR S1 = 1 TO S2
4835 T1 = T1 + G(S1)
4840   NEXT S1
4855   FOR S1 = 1 TO S2
4860 P(S1) = G(S1) / T1
4865   NEXT S1
4880   FOR S1 = 1 TO S2
4885 J(S1) = (S(S1) + L(S1)) * P(S1)
4890   NEXT S1
4905 T2 = 0
4910   FOR S1 = 1 TO S2
4915 T2 = T2 + J(S1)
4920   NEXT S1
4935   FOR S1 = 1 TO S2
4940 PO(S1) = J(S1) / T2
4945   NEXT S1
4960   FOR S1 = 1 TO S2
4965 B(S1) = T1 * PO(S1)
4970   NEXT S1
4985   FOR S1 = 1 TO S2
4990 B(S1) =   INT (B(S1) + .5)
4995   NEXT S1
5010   CALL  - 936
5015   PRINT "BAYESIAN FORECAST"
5020   PRINT : PRINT : PRINT : PRINT : PRINT
5025   FOR S1 = 1 TO S2
5030   PRINT "PY"S1; TAB( 8);B(S1)
5035   NEXT S1
5045   PRINT : PRINT : PRINT : PRINT : PRINT "RETURN TO GO BACK TO MENU"
5050   INPUT ZB$
5055   IF ZB$ = "" GOTO 1040
5065   HOME
5075   PRINT "FACILITY REQUIREMENTS"
5080   PRINT : PRINT : PRINT : PRINT
5085   PRINT "Enter the Department name"
5090   INPUT A1$
5095   PRINT : PRINT "Enter the number per section"
5100   INPUT D
5105   PRINT "Enter the number of courses offered in ";A1$
5110   INPUT X
5115   FOR I = 1 TO X
5120   PRINT "Enter course title"
5125   INPUT B1$(I)
5130   PRINT "Enter the expected enrollment"
5135   INPUT C(I)
5140 Q(I) = C(I) / D
5145 E(I) =   INT (Q(I))
5150 W = (C(I) - (E(I) * D)) / E(I)
5155   IF W > 3 THEN E(I) = E(I) + 1
```

```
5160  PRINT : PRINT "Enter the number of hours class is to   meet per wee
      k."
5165  INPUT F(I)
5170 G(I) = E(I) * F(I)
5175 H(I) = G(I) / 30
5180 H(I) = ( INT ((1000 * H(I)) + .5)) / 1000
5185  HOME
5190  NEXT I
5195  PRINT : PRINT "DEPARTMENT OF ";A1$: PRINT
5200  PRINT "            Enroll-   # of   Hours/  Rooms"
5205  PRINT "Course      ment     sects  week    req."
5210  PRINT
5215  FOR I = 1 TO X
5220  PRINT B1$(I); TAB( 12);C(I); TAB( 22);E(I); TAB( 29);F(I); TAB( 37
      ;H(I)
5225  NEXT I
5230 J = 0
5235  FOR I = 1 TO X
5240 J = J + H(I)
5245  NEXT I
5250 J = ( INT ((100 * J) + .50)) / 100
5255  PRINT  TAB( 36);"-----"
5260  PRINT  TAB( 37);J
5265  PRINT : PRINT : PRINT : PRINT : PRINT "RETURN TO GO BACK TO MENU"
5270  INPUT ZB$
5275  IF ZB$ = "" GOTO 1040
5285  CALL  - 936
5295  PRINT "BREAKING POINT MODEL"
5300  PRINT : PRINT : PRINT : PRINT
5305  PRINT "INPUT NAME OF FIRST CITY:"
5310  INPUT A$
5315  PRINT : PRINT "ENTER NAME OF SECOND CITY:"
5320  INPUT B$
5325  HOME
5330  PRINT "INPUT STUDENT POPULATION IN "A$
5335  INPUT PA
5340  PRINT : PRINT : PRINT : PRINT "INPUT STUDENT POPULATION IN "B$":"
5345  INPUT PB
5350  HOME
5355  PRINT "INPUT DISTANCE BETWEEN "A$" AND "B$" IN MILES;"
5360  INPUT AB
5365  HOME
5370 DB = AB / (1 + ((PA / PB) ^ .5))
5375  PRINT "THE BOUNDARY SHOULD BE DRAWN "DB" MILES FROM THE CENTER OF "
      B$
5380  PRINT : PRINT : PRINT : PRINT : PRINT
5385  PRINT "RETURN TO GO BACK TO MENU"
5390  INPUT ZB$
5395  IF ZB$ = "" GOTO 1040
5405  CALL  - 936
5415  PRINT "LAND USE SCREENING PROC"
5420  PRINT : PRINT : PRINT : PRINT
5425  PRINT "INPUT NUMBER OF SITES TO BE CONSIDERED:"
5430  INPUT J
5435  IF J < 3 THEN JJ = 3
```

```
5440   IF J = 3 OR J > 3 THEN JJ = J.
5445   PRINT : PRINT : FOR I = 1 TO J.
5450   PRINT "ENTER NAME OF SITE "I
5455   INPUT A$(I)
5460   PRINT
5465   NEXT I
5470   HOME
5475   PRINT "ENTER NUMBER.OF CRITERIA TO BE USED:"
5480   INPUT N
5485   PRINT : PRINT : FOR I = 1 TO N
5490   PRINT "ENTER NAME OF CRITERION "I
5495   INPUT B$(I)
5500   PRINT
5505   NEXT I
5510   HOME
5515   FOR S = 1 TO J
5520   FOR I = 1 TO N
5525   PRINT "ENTER RANK ON CRITERION "B$(I)" FOR "A$(S)
5530   INPUT CC(S,I)
5535   HOME
5540   NEXT I
5545   NEXT S
5550   FOR S = 1 TO J
5555   FOR I = 1 TO N
5560 DD(S,I) = 100 - (((100 * CC(S,I)) - 50) / J)
5565   NEXT I
5570   NEXT S
5575   FOR I = 1 TO N
5580   PRINT "ENTER RANK IN IMPORTANCE OF CRITERION "B$(I)
5585   INPUT E(I)
5590   HOME
5595 E(I) = 100 - (((100 * E(I)) - 50) / N)
5600   NEXT I
5605   FOR S = 1 TO J
5610   FOR I = 1 TO N
5615 KK(S,I) = E(I) * DD(S,I)
5620   NEXT I
5625   NEXT S
5630   FOR S = 1 TO J
5635   FOR I = 1 TO N
5640 F(S) = F(S) + KK(S,I)
5645   NEXT I
5650   NEXT S
5655   FOR I = 1 TO N
5660 G = E(I) + G
5665   NEXT I
5670   FOR S = 1 TO J
5675 H(S) = F(S) / G
5680   NEXT S
5685   FOR S = 1 TO J
5690   FOR I = 1 TO N
5695 DD(S,I) = ( INT (DD(S,I) * 5410)) / 10
5700   NEXT I
5705   NEXT S
5710   HOME
```

```
5715   PRINT  TAB( 15);"PERCENTILE RANK PER TOWN"
5720   PRINT "CRITERION"; TAB( 15);A$(1); TAB( 24);A$(2); TAB( 33);A$(3)
5725   FOR I = 1 TO N
5730   PRINT B$(I); TAB( 15);DD(1,I); TAB( 24);DD(2,I); TAB( 33);DD(3,I)
5735   NEXT I
5740   PRINT : PRINT : PRINT
5745   PRINT "SITE"; TAB( 20);"SUITABILITY"
5750   PRINT "----"; TAB( 20);"-----------"
5755   PRINT
5760   FOR S = 1 TO J
5765   PRINT A$(S); TAB( 20);H(S)
5770   NEXT S
5775   PRINT : PRINT : PRINT : PRINT : PRINT "RETURN TO GO BACK TO MENU"
5780   INPUT ZB$
5785   IF ZB$ = "" GOTO 1040
5795   CALL  - 936
5800   FOR I = 1 TO 10
5805   PRINT : NEXT I
5810   PRINT "        PROGRAM COMPLETE"
5815   END
6000   Y(S1) = 0
6010   POKE 216,0
6020   GOTO 3310
6050   Z(S1) = 0
6060   POKE 216,0
6070   GOTO 3355
6100   M(S1) = 0
6110   POKE 216,0
6120   GOTO 3400
6150   L(S1) = 0
6160   POKE 216,0
6170   GOTO 3445
6200   W(S1) = 0
6210   POKE 216,0
6220   GOTO 3265
6250   V(S1) = 0
6260   POKE 216,0
6270   GOTO 3220
6300   U(S1) = 0
6310   POKE 216,0
6320   GOTO 3175
6350   T(S1) = 0
6360   POKE 216,0
6370   GOTO 3130
6400   S(S1) = 0
6410   POKE 216,0
6420   GOTO 3085
6450   R(S1) = 0
6460   POKE 216,0
6470   GOTO 3040
6500   Q(S1) = 0
6510   POKE 216,0
6520   GOTO 2995
```

]

Appendix B
Additional
Problems

The reader should work the problems in this appendix by using the program in Appendix A only after following the suggested "setups" shown in the appropriate chapters. Failure to follow the instructions given earlier in the book will lead to the wrong solutions to the problems.

PROBLEMS RELATED TO CHAPTER 2

Problem 1

Construct an activity network from the following information and find the critical path. This exercise addresses the questions: (A) How long will it take and (B) What activities are critical?

Activities	Time Units
1 ———→ 2	19
2 ———→ 5	14
1 ———→ 3	8
3 ———→ 6	5
1 ———→ 4	17
4 ———→ 6	8
5 ———→ 6	9
6 ———→ 7	17
4 ———→ 8	26
7 ———→ 8	6
8 ———→ 9	10

Answers

A. 75 units
B. 1,2,5,6,7,8,9.

Problem 2

t_e = the average time that an activity would consume if it were repeated many times.

A. From the information below, construct the network and determine the critical path.

Activity	Time Estimates (days)
1 ——> 2	14-20-24
2 ——> 5	9-12-17
1 ——> 3	16-18-20
3 ——> 5	20-24-26
5 ——> 6	4- 6-14
1 ——> 4	7- 8- 9
4 ——> 6	14-18-20

B. The scheduled date of Event 5 is 38 days after the project begins. What is the probability of meeting this date?

Note: This problem may be worked on the microcomputer by connecting activities 1 ——> 2, 2 ——> 5, 1 ——> 3, and 3 ——> 5.

C. What is the probability of completing Event 6 in 47 days?

Note: The entire network as shown in Part A should be used for the microcomputer solution.

Answers

A. 1,3,5,6.

B. $P(Z = -3.05) < .0013$ ($T_E = 41.66$).

C. $P(Z = -.813) = .2091 = .21$ ($T_E = 48.66$); or $P(Z = -.8) = .2119 = .21$. (either answer is acceptable.)

Problem 3

Determine the critical path for the network shown in Figure B.1.

Activity	a	m	b	t_e	v^2
A	.5	1.0	1.5		
B	4	6	12		
C	.5	1.0	1.5		
D	.5	.5	.5		
E	15	17	19		
F	1	3	4		
G	.25	.75	1		

Time Estimates (Months)

Round each z calculation to the nearest tenth.

Figure B.1.   Network for Problem 3 (Chapter 2)

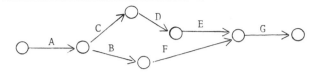

A.   What is the probability of completing the project
     in 21.4 months?
B.   Determine the probability of completing the project
     in 19 months.
C.   Determine the probability of completing the project
     in 20.2 months.
D.   Since the probability of completing the project in
     19 months is very low, discuss some of the ways
     that modifications might be made to improve the
     probability.

Answers

A. $P(z = 1.7) \doteq .9554$ ($T_E = 20.2$).
B. $P(z = -1.7) \doteq .0446$ ($T_E = 20.2$).
C. $P(z = 0) = .5000$.
D.   See Problem 4, Part II.A for suggested procedures
     to improve the probability of completing the
     project.

Problem 4

Develop a solution to a hypothetical problem of
your choice by using PERT according to the following
guidelines.

   I.   A.   Specify the project name and purpose.
        B.   Identify 12 or more activities with 3 time
             estimates each.
        C.   Construct the appropriate network and show
             the critical path.
        D.   Design this network such that the probability
             of completing it on time is low (less than
             20%). This is too low, of course. Therefore,
             your job as a planner is to reduce the criti-
             cal path.
  II.   A.   Now construct a new network from the con-
             straints in Part I according to the follow-
             ing suggestions:
             1.   Reduce the expected time (t_e) of some of
                  the activities on the critical path.
             2.   Transfer some slack time to the critical
                  path.
             3.   Develop parallel activities that may
                  have been in series.
             4.   Request more time if none of the above
                  suggestions can be applied.

B. Design this new network such that the prob-
    ability of completing it on time is better
    than 80 percent. Use the same T_L as applied
    in I above.

III. A. Construct a linear responsibility table for
        the activities in the new network developed
        in Part II. Allow your organization to have
        at least five units (e.g., Board, President,
        etc.) and include at least three levels of
        responsibility (refer to Table 2.1).

Problem 5

The scheduled date of Event 8 is 53 days after the
project begins. Compute the probability of meeting
this date.

Predecessor Event	Successor Event	a	m	b
1	2	7	10	12
2	7	9	12	17
1	3	16	18	20
3	7	20	24	26
7	8	2	3	7
1	4	7	8	9
4	6	14	18	20
1	5	13	15	17
5	6	8	11	13
6	8	25	26	27
4	7	18	25	31

Answer

ΣT_e along the critical path = 51.8333334.
  z = 1.04349838.
  $P(z = 1.04349838) \doteq .85$.

PROBLEMS RELATED TO CHAPTER 3

Problem 1

A. Forecast the expected number of jobs in a given
    region for PY10, PY20, and PY30 if the trend in
    the future is expected to be dependent upon the
    average rate of change over the past 30 years.
    The data set is shown below:

Year	Number of Jobs
-30	4,500
-20	4,600
-10	4,750
Present	4,810

B. Discuss the various assumptions required in the
    above forecasting procedure.

Answer

Year	Number of Jobs
PY10	4,918
PY20	5,029
PY30	5,142

Problem 2

A. The population of a given community 20 years ago
    was 35,000. Ten years ago the population was
    37,500, and presently it is estimated to be 38,900.
    If there are 2.75 persons expected per household,
    how many housing units are needed in the community
    for PY10, PY20, and PY30? There are 14,145 homes
    within the community at present.
B. Over the next 30 years, how many new homes will
    need to be constructed in order to keep pace with
    growth?
C. If the rate of dilapidation is 9 percent, what is
    the total number of new homes needed over the next
    30 years?

Answers

A.

Year	Number of Housing Units
PY10	14,915
PY20	15,726
PY30	16,581

B.

Year	New Homes
PY10	770
PY20	811
PY30	855

C.

Year	Total Number of New Homes
PY10	2,043
PY20	1,969
PY30	1,909

Problem 3

If the total required revenue per student in County
A is $373 and we assume a 6 percent rate of inflation,
what will the total revenue requirements be for PY1
through PY10 if the present and expected student population are as shown below?

Year	Student Population
Present	5,902
PY1	5,900
PY2	5,879
PY3	5,876

PY4	5,890
PY5	5,920
PY6	5,939
PY7	5,968
PY8	5,991
PY9	6,020
PY10	6,032

Answer

Year	Required Revenue per Student		Expected Student Population		Total Revenue Needed
PY1	$395	x	5,900	=	$2,330,500
PY2	419	x	5,879	=	2,463,301
PY3	444	x	5,876	=	2,608,944
PY4	471	x	5,890	=	2,774,190
PY5	499	x	5,920	=	2,954,080
PY6	529	x	5,939	=	3,141,731
PY7	561	x	5,968	=	3,348,048
PY8	595	x	5,991	=	3,564,645
PY9	630	x	6,020	=	3,792,600
PY10	668	x	6,032	=	4,029,376

Problem 4

Seventy-five percent of the total local revenue needed for schools in County A is generated by property taxes. The present property tax rate for schools is $2.90 per $1,000 (.00290) assessed valuation and the assessed property valuation is presently $600 million. If the present assessed valuation is not expected to change over the next ten years, what will the tax rate be per year for PY1 through PY10? (To solve the problem, use the total revenue needed per year as determined in Problem 3 above.)

Answer

Year	75% of Revenue	Rate Required per Year
PY1	$1,747,875	.002913
PY2	1,847,476	.003079
PY3	1,956,708	.003261
PY4	2,080,642	.003468
PY5	2,215,560	.003693
PY6	2,356,298	.003927
PY7	2,511,036	.004185
PY8	2,673,484	.004456
PY9	2,844,450	.004741
PY10	3,022,032	.005037

Problem 5

If County A assumes a bonded indebtedness of $350,000 to be retired in ten years at 6 percent in-

terest with the first payment of principal due in five
years, what will the total revenue needs be for PY1
through PY10?   (In solving this problem, use the
answers determined for Problem 3.)

Answer

Year	Total Revenue Needed
PY1	$2,351,500
PY2	2,484,301
PY3	2,629,944
PY4	2,795,190
PY5	3,033,413
PY6	3,217,564
PY7	3,420,381
PY8	3,633,478
PY9	3,857,933
PY10	4,091,209

PROBLEMS RELATED TO CHAPTER 4

Problem 1

Forecast five years of resident live births from
the five consecutive years presented below. Assume
rather consistent economic conditions and use the standard compound interest formula to complete the forecast.

Year	RLB
-4	1,287
-3	1,298
-2	1,321
-1	1,325
Present	1,331

Answer

Year	Resident Live Births
PY1	1,342
PY2	1,354
PY3	1,365
PY4	1,377
PY5	1,388

Problem 2

Background.   You are the senior educational planner
for Bogie County, Florida. The principal of Par Elementary School has requested that you make a five-year projection of student enrollment in her school. The hard
data that you need are

1. Resident live births in the county for the
    past ten years.

2.   Net enrollment data by grade for the past five
     years.

     Data.   To obtain resident live births, you contact
the Bureau of Vital Statistics in Tallahassee.   The RLBs
for Bogie County six years before enrollment in grade 1
are as follows:

Year	RLB
-4	1,220
-3	1,226
-2	1,234
-1	1,248
Present	1,301
PY1	1,312
PY2	1,316
PY3	1,305
PY4	1,300
PY5	1,320

Net enrollment data, as given below, are available in
the office of the Bogie County Superintendent of
Schools.

Grade	-4 Years	-3 Years	-2 Years	-1 Year	Present
1	402	428	431	451	468
2	417	415	434	446	452
3	420	420	430	439	447
Total	1,239	1,263	1,295	1,336	1,367

     Problem.   Forecast the student population by grade
level for Par Elementary School for five consecutive
years (PY1 through PY5).

Answer

Grade	PY1	PY2	PY3	PY4	PY5
1	459	460	456	455	462
2	478	468	470	466	464
3	458	485	475	477	473
Total	1,395	1,413	1,401	1,398	1,399

Problem 3

     Forecast the total enrollment (PY1 through PY5)
for the data base presented in Problem 2 as follows:

A.   Calculate the forecast with the SCI model.
B.   Determine the forecast by employing the
     regression formula.

Answer

A. | Year | Enrollment |
    |------|-----------|
    | PY1 | 1,401 |
    | PY2 | 1,436 |
    | PY3 | 1,472 |
    | PY4 | 1,508 |
    | PY5 | 1,546 |

B. PYN = 1,201.3 + 32.9X
    PY1 = 1,399
    PY2 = 1,432
    PY3 = 1,465
    PY4 = 1,497
    PY5 = 1,530
    SE = ± 3.896

Problem 4

Develop a five-year Bayesian forecast for the total enrollment data presented in Problem 2 as follows:

Step 1: Allow the total forecast per year in Problem 2 to be the prior distribution.
Step 2: Let Problems 3.A and 3.B be the sample distribution.
Step 3: Compute the posterior distribution. Multiply each independent component of the posterior distribution by the grand total of Problem 2.

Answer

Year	Enrollment
PY1	1,330
PY2	1,380
PY3	1,401
PY4	1,430
PY5	1,465

Problem 5

Determine the regression formula for the following enrollment data:

Year	Enrollment
-9	84
-8	85
-7	102
-6	100
-5	81
-4	87
-3	95
-2	72
-1	91
Present	82

Answer

PYN = 92.4 - .82X.
SE = ± 8.4.

Problem 6

Substitute X = 11, 12, ..., 20 in the formula determined from the above data. The result is the regression
forecast for ten years.

Answer

Year	Enrollment	Year	Enrollment
PY1	83	PY6	79
PY2	83	PY7	78
PY3	82	PY8	78
PY4	81	PY9	77
PY5	80	PY10	76

Problem 7

Determine a five-year forecast for the enrollment
data presented below:

Grade	-4 Years	-3 Years	-2 Years	-1 Year	Present
1	248	290	245	239	267
2	250	259	272	228	214
3	270	260	252	266	214
4	280	261	253	267	215
5	281	262	254	268	216
6	282	263	255	269	217
7	283	264	256	270	218
8	284	265	257	271	219
9	285	266	258	272	220
10	286	267	259	273	221
11	287	268	260	274	222
12	288	269	261	275	223

The resident live births six years before enrollment in
grade 1 are as follows:

Year	RLB
-4	815
-3	813
-2	708
-1	699
Present	758
PY1	729
PY2	692
PY3	577
PY4	568
PY5	552

Answer

Grade	PY1	PY2	PY3	PY4	PY5
1	248	235	196	193	188
2	254	236	224	187	184

Grade	PY1	PY2	PY3	PY4	PY5
3	210	250	232	220	184
4	204	200	238	221	210
5	203	192	189	224	209
6	204	192	182	178	212
7	205	193	181	172	169
8	206	194	182	171	162
9	207	195	183	172	162
10	208	196	184	173	163
11	209	197	185	174	164
12	210	198	186	175	165

PROBLEMS RELATED TO CHAPTER 5

Answers are not provided for these problems, since each student may assume a different basic educational program.

Problem 1

Develop a basic educational program for grades K-6 over a ten-year period. Assume the following enrollments:

Present	650	PY6	711
PY1	655	PY7	698
PY2	669	PY8	684
PY3	684	PY9	680
PY4	692	PY10	675
PY5	704		

Assume 25 students per section and determine the acceptable space requirements by consulting the minimum standards for your state (See Tables 5.1 and 5.2 for examples).

Problem 2

Determine the gross square feet required by your program. If the cost of construction and furnishings is $48 per square foot, what will the cost of the new facility be?

Problem 3

If the site for the new elementary school is $2 million, what is the total cost of the new facility excluding interest over ten years?

Problem 4

Assume a 12 percent rate of interest, determine a payback schedule over a ten-year period and calculate the total cost for the site, furnishings, and facility. You may use the following rate schedule: $(1.12)^1$ = interest rate for PY1; $(1.12)^2$ = interest rate for PY2; $(1.12)^3$ = interest rate for PY3, and so forth.

The microcomputer program, "Payback Schedule" is suggested.

PROBLEMS RELATED TO CHAPTER 6

Problem 1

Two population centers located 15 miles apart and
within the same school district have received a mandate
to establish new boundary lines and modify their attendance zones because existing facilities have been improved. The following survey data are provided:

	Town A	Town B
Student population (K-12)	1096	1781
Capacity of Facilities (K-12)	1200	1900

Assuming that the population densities of the two towns
are about equal and that access routes are equal,
determine where the new boundary should be located.

Answer

d_A = 6.59 miles.
d_B = 8.41 miles.

Problem 2

Because of recent population expansion, expected
growth, and inadequate and condemned facilities for
grade levels K-9, two population centers have agreed
to build a new educational complex appropriate for
their expected student populations (K-9) at least 20
years into the future. The centers are ten miles apart;
there are no significant natural barriers in the region.
Access at any point between the two centers is good.
Determine where the new educational complex should be
located if the K-9 student population 20 years from now
is expected to be 650 for Town A and 450 for Town B.

Answer

d_A = 4.54 miles.
d_B = 5.46 miles.

Problem 3

Cities A and B, 12 miles apart, are competing for
a community college complex to be located within their
city limits. Since accessibility for each city is
equal, the locational criteria to be used are distance,
availability, and population 20 years from now. Where
should the community college be located?
The following data are available.

DISTANCE: From the center of City A to the center of
    City B the distance is 12 miles.

AVAILABILITY:

Criterion	Score	City A	City B
Available land	170	x	x
Public library	150	x	x
Gymnasium	100	x	
Soccer fields	75		x
Football field	60		x
Site adjacent to public park	50		x
Site adjacent to lake	40	x	

POPULATION (16 years and older):

	City A	City B
PY10	7,200	8,100
PY20	12,800	10,900

The total scores that have been assigned to the three major location criteria are 200 for distance, 150 for availability, and 300 for population.

Answer

City A is the better location.

Problem 4

By adding cost of land (150 acres) to the location criteria in Problem 3, determine which city should be selected. The major criterion scores are distance, 200; availability, 150; population, 300; and cost, 350. Furthermore, the alternative sites of 300 acres and their costs are in City A, $2.6 million, and City B, $2.5 million.

Answer

City B is the better location.

Problem 5

The results of a Delphi analysis concerning the appropriate site for a new coliseum designed to serve towns A, B, and C reveal the criteria are availability, population, and distance. Selection will depend on the scores from the Delphi study and the information shown below:

Score	Rank		Score	A	B	C
(206)	( )	Availability				
		Bus Service	(218)	x	x	–
		Space Available Adjacent to Park	(138)	–	x	x
		Air Service	(157)	x	–	–
		Train Service	(82)	–	x	x
		Rank		( )	( )	( )

(208)   (   )   <u>Population</u>

                    A - 46,000
                    B - 42,000
                    C - 44,000

(178)   (   )   <u>Distance</u>

                    AB - 13 miles
                    AC - 17 miles
                    BC - 15 miles

Which site is best?

Answer

City A is the better location.

Appendix C
Formula
Proofs

DERIVATION OF BREAKING POINT MODELS

Each center of population P, of towns A and B will attract students directly according to the size of their respective population, $P_A \div P_B$, and inversely with respect to the square of the relative distance, $(d_B \div d_A)^2$, from a point between the two centers. Any point between the two centers of population may be determined as follows:

$$d_A + d_B = d_{AB}.$$

$$d_A = d_{AB} - d_B, \text{ or}$$

$$d_B = d_{AB} - d_B,$$

where d_A is the distance from A to the point where the forces are equalized and likewise for d_B. The distance between A and B is d_{AB} and the relationship between population size and distance is

$$\frac{P_A}{P_B} \left[\frac{d_B}{d_A} \right]^2 = 1.$$

Multiply in each side of the equation by

$$\left[\frac{d_A}{d_B} \right]^2$$

To find the distance from B to the boundary or breaking point, substitute $d_{AB} - d_B$ for d_A. Thus

$$\frac{P_A}{P_B} = \left[\frac{d_{AB} - d_B}{d_B} \right]^2 \; ,$$

and taking the square root of each side we determine that:

$$\sqrt{\frac{P_A}{P_B}} = \frac{d_{AB} - d_B}{d_B} \; .$$

The solution for d_B is determined as follows:

$$d_B \left(\sqrt{\frac{P_A}{P_B}} \right) = d_{AB} - d_B$$

$$d_B + d_B \left(\sqrt{\frac{P_A}{P_B}} \right) = d_{Ab}$$

$$d_B \left[1 + \sqrt{\frac{P_A}{P_B}} \right] = d_{AB}, \; \text{and}$$

$$d_B = \frac{d_{AB}}{1 + \sqrt{\frac{P_A}{P_B}}} \; .$$

By following a similar routine d_A may be determined as illustrated below:

$$\frac{P_A}{P_B} = \left[\frac{d_A}{d_B} \right]^2 \quad \text{or}$$

$$\left[\frac{d_A}{d_B} \right]^2 = \frac{P_A}{P_B} \; .$$

Step 1 $\left[\dfrac{d_A}{d_{AB} - d_A}\right]^2 = \dfrac{P_A}{P_B}$.

Step 2 $\dfrac{d_A}{d_{AB} - d_A} = \sqrt{\dfrac{P_A}{P_B}}$,

Step 3 $d_A = \left[d_{AB} - d_A\right]\sqrt{\dfrac{P_A}{P_B}}$,

Step 4 $d_A = d_{AB}\sqrt{\dfrac{P_A}{P_B}} - d_A\sqrt{\dfrac{P_A}{P_B}}$,

Step 5 $d_A + d_A\sqrt{\dfrac{P_A}{P_B}} = d_{AB}\sqrt{\dfrac{P_A}{P_B}}$,

Step 6 $d_A\left[1 + \sqrt{\dfrac{P_A}{P_B}}\right] = d_{AB}\sqrt{\dfrac{P_A}{P_B}}$,

Step 7 $d_A = \dfrac{d_{AB}\sqrt{\dfrac{P_A}{P_B}}}{1 + \sqrt{\dfrac{P_A}{P_B}}}$.

   These formulae are designed to allow the largest population center to extend its attraction farther than the smaller center. The inverse of this result is needed when site location is being considered.

THE SITE LOCATION FORMULA: REILLY'S LAW

   To determine a set of formulae for site location, it is obvious that the inverse solutions to the above formulae would yield the desired result. Hence in site location between two population centers it is clear that the larger population center will have the strong-

est attraction. As a result, the proposed site should
be closer to the larger population center.

The distance from center B is determined as follows,
given $d_A + d_B = d_{AB}$, and

$$\frac{P_A}{P_B} \left[\frac{d_A}{d_B} \right]^2 = 1, \text{ or}$$

$$\left[\frac{d_A}{d_B} \right]^2 = \frac{P_B}{P_A} \, .$$

Step 1 $$\frac{d_A}{d_B} = \sqrt{\frac{P_B}{P_A}} \, ,$$

Step 2 $$\frac{d_{AB} - d_B}{d_B} = \sqrt{\frac{P_B}{P_A}} \, ,$$

Step 3 $$d_{AB} - d_B = d_B \sqrt{\frac{P_B}{P_A}} \, ,$$

Step 4 $$d_{AB} = d_B + d_B \sqrt{\frac{P_B}{P_A}} \, ,$$

Step 5 $$d_{AB} = d_B \left[1 + \sqrt{\frac{P_B}{P_A}} \right]$$

Step 6 $$d_B \left[1 + \sqrt{\frac{P_B}{P_A}} \right] = d_{AB} \, ,$$

Step 7 $$d_B = \frac{d_{AB}}{1 + \sqrt{\frac{P_B}{P_A}}} \, .$$

Appendix D
School Plant
Evaluation Forms

A set of four evaluation forms is included here. This set, provided by Dr. C. W. McGuffey, the University of Georgia, illustrates site and building components that should be evaluated. The first form may be used to prepare a statistical overview of the school system, which may be inventoried in more detail with the second form. The last two forms are for site and building evaluation.

SCHOOL PLANT EVALUATION

School System: _____   Date: _____

School Name: _____   Evaluator: _____

SCHOOL PLANT DATA:

1. Site Size: _____

2. No. of Site Parcels: _____

3. No. Buildings on Site: _____

4. Age of Buildings: _____

5. Current Active Enrollment for Each Grade:

   K _____   5 _____   10 _____   Special Education: _____
   1 _____   6 _____   11 _____   Total: _____
   2 _____   7 _____   12 _____
   3 _____   8 _____
   4 _____   9 _____   Total _____

6. Total Number of Instructional Rooms: _____

7. Number of Unsatisfactory Instructional Rooms: _____

8. Number of Portables and/or Relocateables: _____

9. Estimated Pupil Capacity of School Plant: _____

Note: Used by permission of Dr. C. W. McGuffey, University of Georgia.

SCHOOL PLANT INVENTORY

School Center _____ Est. Cap. _____ Grades _____ Current Enrollment _____

Type of Space	Number of Standard Spaces		No. of Substandard Spaces Used In				Capacity*
	Used	Unused	Improvised Space Perm. Bldgs.	Relocate-ables	Non-Pub. Owned	Obsolete Bldgs.	
Clrms. @ 30 pupils							
Clrms. @ pupils							
Science							
Homemaking							
Ind. Arts Shops							
Special Edr.							
Industrial Shops							
Book Rooms							
Storage							
Agriculture							
Bus. Ed. (Labs)							
Drawing							

Music					
Art					
Gymnatorium or Gymnasium					
Shower & Locker Rooms					
Cafetorium or Lunchroom					
Library					
Auditorium					
Admin. Suite					
Toilets					
Pupil Personnel Services					

* Capacity assigned should take into consideration (1) size of classroom, (2) pupil stations in special facilities, and (3) teacher stations.

Note: Used by permission of Dr. C. W. McGuffey, University of Georgia.

Site Evaluation

School Name: _____   Evaluator: _____

Parcel No: _____   Date: _____

Item	Criteria			Scale*		
		1	2	3	4	5
1. Size:	Elementary: 10 acres plus one acre for each one hundred pupils. Middle: 20 acres plus one acre for each one hundred pupils. Senior High: 30 acres plus one acre for each one hundred pupils.	1	2	3	4	5
2. Drainage	Water drains readily from the site without creating site erosion.	1	2	3	4	5
3. Safety	Pedestrian walkways and vehicular drives do not cross but provide for safe ingress and exit to and from the site.	1	2	3	4	5
4. Accessibility	Site is located central to the pupils it serves and is relatively easy to get to over access roads, streets and sidewalks.	1	2	3	4	5
5. Parking	The parking space provided is paved, lighted and adequate for both cars and bicycles allowed by school policy.	1	2	3	4	5
6. Environment	The environs of the school site are free of dust, noises, odors, unsightly conditions and undesirable neighbors that distract from the functions of the school.	1	2	3	4	5

		1	2	3	4	5
7.	Landscaping — Grounds around buildings and in court areas are sodded and plantings around buildings and along walks and drives are attractive and well kept.	1	2	3	4	5
8.	Playground/ Athletic Fields — Playgrounds and athletic fields are organized and well defined and are adequate for the program. Needed outdoor lighting is provided.	1	2	3	4	5
9.	Land Use — Land assigned to the school is properly developed and available for use in the school's program. Non-usable land is minimal.	1	2	3	4	5
10.	Utilities — All needed utilities are available for use by the school.	1	2	3	4	5
11.	Terrain — Land is generally sloping and convex in shape. Elevation differences are minimal.	1	2	3	4	5
12.	Fencing — Appropriate fencing is provided to promote control, safety and security of pupils and property.	1	2	3	4	5

*The five level rating scale is as follows: (1) Missing--The feature is needed but nonexistent. (2) Inadequate--The feature is present but clearly impedes the functioning of the process it purports to support. Criteria clearly are not met. (3) Marginal--The feature does not meet criteria. The level of adequacy permits limited use, but performance is restricted. (4) Adequate--The feature clearly meets established criteria and is functioning well. (5) Superior--The feature clearly exceeds established criteria, and the level of performance exceeds expectations. A rating of 48-60 indicates an adequate to superior site; 24-48, a marginal site; and 12-24, an inadequate site.

Note: Used by permission of Dr. C. W. McGuffey, University of Georgia.

Individual Building Evaluation

Name of School: _____   Building Name or Number: _____   Date: _____

Date of Construction: _____

	Component	Criteria	Scale*				
1.	Structure	The structure is of fire-resistive or non-combustible construction and allows interior convertibility and exterior expansion. The structure is in sound condition.	1	2	3	4	5
2.	Exterior Walls	The exterior walls are in good condition and materials are easily maintained.	1	2	3	4	5
3.	Roofing	The roof drains well and is in good condition.	1	2	3	4	5
4.	Fenestration	Windows are free of air leakage, in good condition and are adequately shielded from glare. Minimum window area requirements are provided.	1	2	3	4	5
5.	Interior Partitions	Interior partitions are in good condition, are non-load bearing and may be relocated with a minimum of labor and expense. Finishes enhance lighting and appearance.	1	2	3	4	5
6.	Floors	Floor materials provide acoustical control and are economically maintained.	1	2	3	4	5
7.	Sanitary System	Sanitary fixtures are adequate in number for the school population and are in good condition.	1	2	3	4	5

		1	2	3	4	5
8.	Plumbing System	Water supply and waste water facilities meet school requirements. City water and sanitary sewer are provided. Plumbing is in good condition.				
9.	Electrical/ Electronic System	Electrical supply is adequate to all rooms and spaces of the school without overloading the system. The school is supplied with electrical clocks, intercom and bell system.				
10.	Ceiling	Ceiling is of acoustical materials and painted a light shade of off-white color. Finish is in good condition.				
11.	Safety Facilities	Safety lights and exit signs are provided. A fire detection and alarm system are in good working order. All exit hardware is panic type and free of locks. On multi-story buildings stairwells are enclosed and stairwell and corridor materials are one-hour fire rated.				
12.	Artificial Lighting	Artificial light sources supply at least 30 foor candles of glare free light at desk top level. Fixtures are clean, in good condition and provide for maximum operating efficiency. (Watts per square foot:)				

*The five level rating scale is as follows: (1) <u>Missing</u>--The feature is needed but nonexistent. (2) <u>Inadequate</u>--The feature is present but clearly impedes the functioning of the process it purports to support. Criteria clearly are not met. (3) <u>Marginal</u>--The feature does not meet criteria. The level of adequacy permits limited use, but performance is restricted. (4) <u>Adequate</u>--The feature clearly meets established criteria and is functioning well. (5) <u>Superior</u>--The feature clearly exceeds established criteria, and the level of performance exceeds expectations. A rating of 66-90 indicates an adequate to superior building; 42-66, a marginal building; and 18-42, an inadequate building.

Note: Used by permission of Dr. C. W. McGuffey, University of Georgia.

Individual Building Evaluation (Cont'd)

Name of School: _____

Building Name or Number: _____

Component	Criteria	Scale*				
		1	2	3	4	5
13. Insulation	Building shell is insulated so that maximum energy conservation is attained. (U Factor: Roof -.06; Walls -.10)	1	2	3	4	5
14. Heating System	The heating system is adequate to maintain all occupied instructional and work areas at 68° Fahrenheit. Heating controls, time clocks and room thermostats are in good working order.	1	2	3	4	5
15. Ventilation	An adequate air supply is available to remove stale air and odors from occupied areas and noxious fumes and odors from shops and laboratories.	1	2	3	4	5
16. Air Conditioning	Cooling is supplied to all instructional areas so that temperatures are maintained at no more than 78° Fahrenheit.	1	2	3	4	5
17. Accessibility	All floors, areas and facilities can be reached by persons who are on crutches, in wheelchairs, or are otherwise disabled.	1	2	3	4	5
18. Building Equipment	All built-in or installed operating equipment, millwork and cabinet work are functional, efficient and in good condition.	1	2	3	4	5

Notes

CHAPTER 1. INTRODUCTION TO PLANNING
CONCEPTS AND MICROCOMPUTERS

1. E. S. Quade, <u>Analysis for Public Decisions</u> (New York: Elsevier North Holland, 1979).

2. D. Adams and R. N. Bjork, <u>Education in Developing Areas</u> (New York: D. McKay, 1969); A. Anderson and M. J. Bourman, "Theoretical Consideration in Educational Planning," in D. Adams, Ed., <u>Educational Planning</u> (Syracuse, N.Y.: Syracuse University Press, 1964).

3. R. Diez-Hochleitner, "Educational Planning," <u>Economics and Social Aspects of Educational Planning</u> (Paris: UNESCO, 1964).

4. D. E. Inbar, "Educational Planning: A Review and a Plea," <u>Review of Educational Research</u> 50 (Fall 1980): 377-92.

5. Amitai Etzioni, "Mixed Scanning: A Third Approach to Decision-Making," <u>Public Administration Review</u> 27 (December 1967): 385-92.

6. Charles E. Lindbloom, "The Science of Muddling Through," <u>Public Administration Review</u> 19 (1959): 79-88.

7. Burt Nanus, "Interdisciplinary Policy Analysis in Economic Forecasting," <u>Technological Forecasting and Social Change</u> no. 4 (May 1979): 285.

8. Charles E. Lindbloom, <u>The Policy-Making Process</u> (Englewood Cliffs, N.J.: Prentice-Hall, 1968), 4.

9. Quade, <u>Analysis for Public Decisions</u>, 22.

10. Charles O. Jones, <u>An Introduction to the Study of Public Policy</u>, 2nd ed. (North Scituate, Mass.: Duxbury, 1977).

11. Lindbloom, <u>The Policy-Making Process</u>.

12. Peter W. House, <u>The Art of Public Policy Analysis</u> (Beverly Hills: Sage Publications, 1982), 238.

13. Hugh Heclo, "Policy Analysis," <u>British Journal of Political Science</u> 15 (January 1972): 85.

14. Articles on planning may be found in the following journals: <u>Planning and Changing</u> (Normal, Ill.: Department of Educational Administration and Foundations, Illinois State University); <u>Socio-Economic Planning Sciences</u> (Elmsford, N.Y.: Pergamon Press, Maxwell

House; or Oxford: Headington Hill Hall); <u>Technological Forecasting and Social Change</u> (New York: Elsevier North Holland, Inc.); <u>Policy Studies Journal</u> (Urbana, Ill.: University of Illinois); <u>Journal of the American Planning Association</u> (Washington, D.C.: American Planning Association); <u>Futures</u> (Guildford, Surrey, Eng.: IPC Science and Technology Press, Ltd.); <u>The Futurist</u> (Washington, D.C.: World Future Society). Planning literature is also published by the Council of Educational Facility Planners, International, 29 West Woodruff Avenue, Columbus, Ohio, 43210.

15. Barclay M. Hudson, "Comparison of Current Planning Theories: Counterparts and Contradictions," <u>Journal of the American Planning Association</u> no. 4 (October 1979): <u>387-98</u>.

16. John Friedman, <u>Retracking America: A Theory of Transactive Planning</u> (Garden City, N.Y.: Doubleday, 1973).

17. Daniel Friedman, "Towards Professional Literacy in Educational Computing," <u>Educational Computer Magazine</u> no. 6 (November/December 1982): 28-29.

18. W. L. Somervell, Jr., "Survival in the High-Technology Era," <u>Technological Horizons in Education Journal</u> no. 5 (March 1983): <u>90</u>.

19. Dorothy H. Judd, "Teacher Created Programs: Suggestions for Success," <u>Educational Computer Magazine</u> no. 6 (November/December 1982): <u>34</u>.

20. Todd Hoover and Sandra Gould, "Computerizing the School Office: The Hidden Cost," <u>NASSP Bulletin</u> no. 455 (September 1982): 34.

21. Arthur S. Melmed, "Information Technology for U.S. Schools," <u>Phi Delta Kappan</u> no. 5 (January 1982): 308.

22. Karen Sheingold, Janet H. Kane, and Mari E. Endreweit, "Microcomputer Use in Schools: Developing a Research Agenda," <u>Harvard Educational Review</u> 53 (November 1983): 412-32.

CHAPTER 2. TIME MANAGEMENT AND SCHEDULING METHODS

1. Willard Fox and Alfred Schwartz, <u>Managerial Guide for School Principals</u> (Columbus, Ohio: Charles E. Merrill Books, 1965), 59-73.

2. Joseph D. Cooper, <u>Hot To Get More Done in Less Time</u> (Garden City, N.Y.: Doubleday, 1971).

3. Peter F. Drucker, <u>The Effective Executive</u> (New York: Harper and Row, 1967).

4. George S. Odiorne, <u>Management by Objectives: A System of Managerial Leadership</u> (New York: Pitman, 1965); Peter F. Drucker, <u>The Practice of Management</u> (New York: Harper and Row, 1954).

5. C. Kenneth Tanner and Earl J. Williams, Educational <u>Planning and Decision Making</u> (Lexington, Mass.: D.C. Heath, 1981), 81-109.

6. Fred Pryor, <u>Managing Time</u> (Shawnee Mission, Kansas: Fred Pryor Seminars, 1976).

7. James L. Hager and L. E. Scarr, <u>It's About Time</u> (Kirkland, Wash.: Management Development Associates, 1978), 27.

8. Gerald A. Silver, <u>Introduction to Management</u> (St. Paul, Minn.: West Publishing, 1981), 35.

9. Frank W. Banghart, Educational Systems Analysis (Toronto: Collier-Macmillan Canada, 1969), 151-52.

10. Guilbert C. Hentschke, Management Operations in Education (Berkeley: McCutchan Publishing Corp., 1975), 261-75.

11. Edward L. Hannan, "The Application of Goal Programming Techniques to the CPM Problem," Socio-Economic Planning Sciences 12, no. 5 (1978): 267.

12. Department of the Navy, Bureau of Naval Weapons, Program Evaluation Research Task Summary Report Phase 2 (0-584982), Special Projects Office (Washington, D.C.: U.S. Government Printing Office, 1958), 1-2.

13. Ibid., 1.

14. Ibid., 1-2.

CHAPTER 3. METHODS OF COMMUNITY, REGIONAL, AND ECONOMIC ANALYSIS

1. Kenneth W. Brooks, Marion C. Conrad, and William Griffith, From Program to Educational Facilities (Lexington, Ky.: Center for Professional Development, College of Education, University of Kentucky, 1980), 68.

2. Herbert Hyman, Survey Design and Analysis (New York: Free Press, 1967).

3. Seymour Sudman, Reducing the Cost of Surveys (Chicago: Aldine, 1967).

4. Fred N. Kerlinger, Foundations of Behavioral Research (New York: Holt, Rinehart and Winston, 1967).

5. Carter V. Good, Introduction to Educational Research (New York: Appleton-Century-Crofts, 1963).

6. Robert P. Hagemann and Thomas J. Espenshade, "The Impact of Changing State Economic Conditions of Public School Enrollments," Socio-Economic Planning Sciences 13, no. 5 (1979): 268.

7. Daniel C. Rogers and Hirsch S. Ruchlin, Economics and Education (New York: The Free Press, 1971), 212-17.

8. W. Arthur Lewis, "Economic Development with Unlimited Supplies of Labor," Manchester School of Economic and Social Studies 22 (1954), and John Fei and Gustav Ranis, Development of the Labor Surplus Economy: Theory and Practice (Homewood, Ill.: Richard D. Irwin, 1964), as discussed by Rogers and Ruchlin, Economics and Education, 217-19.

9. Roe L. Johns and Edgar L. Morphet, The Economics and Financing of Education (Englewood Cliffs, N.J.: Prentice-Hall, 1975), 142-77.

10. Charles S. Benson, The Economics of Public Education (Boston: Houghton Mifflin, 1978), 261-91.

11. Dewey H. Stollar, Managing School Indebtedness (Danville, Ill.: Interstate Printers and Publishers, 1967).

CHAPTER 4. POPULATION FORECASTING MODELS

1. Robert P. Hagemann and Thomas J. Espenshade, "The Impact of Changing State Economic Conditions on Public School Enrollments,"

Socio-Economic Planning Sciences 13, no. 5 (1979): 265-73.

2. Gary G. Breegle, "Socio-economic Variables Which Discriminate Between Increasing and Decreasing Enrollments Among Tennessee Public School Districts," Ph.D. diss., University of Tennessee, Knoxville, 1979), 68-69.

3. Russell G. Davis and Gary M. Lewis, "The Demographic Background to Changing Enrollments and School Needs," in Susan Abramowitz and Stuart Rosenfeld, Eds., *Declining Enrollments: The Challenge of the Coming Decade* (Washington, D.C.: U.S. Department of Health, Education, and Welfare, 1978), 19-46.

4. Ellen Bussard and Alan C. Green, *Planning for Declining Enrollment in Single High School Districts* (Washington, D.C.: U.S. Department of Education, 1981), 1-2.

5. George J. Greenawalt and Donald P. Mitchell, *Predicting School Enrollments* (Cambridge, Mass.: New England School Development Council, 1966), 20-21.

6. Hagemann and Espenshade, "The Impact of Changing State Economic Conditions," 268.

7. Ibid., 266.

8. C. Kenneth Tanner, *Designs for Educational Planning* (Lexington, Mass.: D.C. Heath, 1971), 32-39.

CHAPTER 5. PLANNING AND MANAGEMENT METHODS
FOR PROGRAM, FACILITIES, AND ENERGY

1. Roger A. Kaufman, *Educational System Planning* (Englewood Cliffs, N.J.: Prentice-Hall, 1972).

2. Lee Boone, Meade Guy, and Jackie Walsh, *A Planning Primer for Local Educators* (Montgomery, Ala.: Alabama State Department of Education, Office of Planning and Evaluation, 1977).

3. Kenneth W. Brooks, Marion C. Conrad, and William Griffith, *From Program to Educational Facilities* (Lexington, Ky.: University of Kentucky, Center for Professional Development, 1980), 29-38.

4. A classic reference on selecting and initiating a central survey committee is Merle R. Sumption, *How To Conduct a Citizens School Survey* (New York: Prentice-Hall, 1952).

5. C. Kenneth Tanner and Earl J. Williams, *Educational Planning and Decision Making* (Lexington, Mass.: D.C. Heath, 1981), 81-109.

6. Ibid., 111-23.

7. Basil Castaldi, "The School Building Survey," in *Educational Facilities: Planning, Remodeling, and Management* (Boston: Allyn and Bacon, 1977); Carol McGuffey, *Model for the Evaluation of Educational Buildings* (Chicago: Chicago Board of Education, 1974).

8. Nickolaus L. Engelhardt, *Complete Guide for Planning New Schools* (West Nyack, N.Y.: Parker Publishing Company, 1970), 30-36.

9. *Rules, Regulations and Minimum Standards (1979-1980)* (Nashville: Tennessee State Board of Education), 91-111.

CHAPTER 6. BOUNDARY AND SITE LOCATION MODELS

1. Mark S. Henry, "The Spatial and Temporal Economic Impact of a Nuclear Energy Center--A Methodological Discourse and Application

to a Southern Regional Site," <u>Socio-Economic Planning Sciences</u> 15, no. 2 (1981): 59-64.

2.   D. Mulkey and J. Hite, "A Procedure for Estimating Inter-regional Input-Output Matrices from Secondary Data," <u>Technical Bulletin</u> 1072 (Clemson, S.C.: South Carolina Agricultural Experiment Station, 1979).

3.   Henry, "Spatial and Temporal Economic Impact of a Nuclear Energy Center," 59-60.

4.   M. Cordey-Hays and A. G. Wilson, "Spatial Interaction," <u>Socio-Economic Planning Sciences</u> 5, no. 1 (1971): 73-95.

5.   M. Cordey-Hays, "Dynamic Frameworks for Spatial Models," <u>Socio-Economic Planning Sciences</u> 6, no. 4 (1972): 365-85.

6.   Donald A. Krueckeberg and Arthur L. Silvers, <u>Urban Planning Analysis: Methods and Models</u> (New York: John Wiley and Sons, 1974), 288-317.

7.   William J. Reilly, "Methods for the Study of Retail Relationships," <u>University of Texas Bulletin</u> 2944 (1929). As presented by Krueckeberg and Silvers, <u>Urban Planning Analysis</u>, 288-317.

8.   Krueckeberg and Silvers, <u>Urban Planning and Analysis</u>, 292-94.

9.   Jerome E. Dobson, <u>The Maryland Power Plant Siting Project: An Application of the ORNL Land Use Screening Procedure</u> (Oak Ridge, Tenn.: Oak Ridge National Laboratory, 1977).

10.   Fadia M. Alvic, "A Mathematical Site Selection Procedure for Future College Locations, Including an Analysis of Community College Geographic Locations Within 34 States," (Ph.D. diss., The University of Tennessee, Knoxville, 1981).

11.   Henry E. Garrett, <u>Statistics in Psychology and Education</u> (New York: David McKay Company, 1965), 68-69.

12.   Kenneth W. Brooks, Marion C. Conrad, and William Griffith, <u>From Program to Educational Facilities</u> (Lexington, Ky.: Center for Professional Development, University of Kentucky College of Education, 1980).

13.   <u>Guide for Planning Educational Facilities</u> (Columbus, Ohio: Council of Educational Facilities Planners, International, 1979).

About the Authors

C. Kenneth Tanner is Associate Professor of Educational Administration and Coordinator of Graduate Programs, Bureau of Educational Studies, at the University of Georgia. He is the former president of the International Society for Educational Planning and has served on the Task Force on Technological Forecasting. He is a consultant for government, education, and industry. Dr. Tanner is a graduate of the Florida State University. He has been a public school administrator and teacher in junior high and high school.

C. Thomas Holmes is Assistant Professor of Educational Administration, College of Education and the Graduate School, the University of Georgia. He is a graduate of the University of Georgia. His areas of expertise include educational research, school personnel, and microcomputer technology. Dr. Holmes has also been a high school science teacher.

Index